1

This book is available for sale on Amazon and www.CrownandClothCo.com

ISBN: 979-8-9866720-2-1

For Worldwide Distribution, Printed in the U.S.A.

How to Deal:

A Skeptics Walk with Christ Through the Wilderness

Desirée L. Jones

Table of Contents

How to Deal: *A Skeptic's Walk with Christ Through the Wilderness*

Dedication

To those who feel less than worthy of the love of God
To those who have felt outcast from the "Church"
To those who have turned away from God due to the pain
inflicted by false teachings

To my mother, Heather, who has always been my example
of the agape love of God
To my dear friend, Teresa, who has been a constant
support and encouragement and the shoulders on which I
stand
To my husband, Dr. CJ, who has encouraged and guided
me through this journey of discovery with love and grace
and most importantly, lots and lots of patience

How to Deal: *A Skeptic's Walk with Christ Through the Wilderness*

Prologue

As a young adult who had always shown an interest in God, but also had my own eccentric style and personality, I never felt accepted in the church. Before I was even able to get to the point of opening up and reading a Bible for myself, I was run off by these Christians who told me I was not accepted the way I am simply because I didn't look, speak, and act like them.

My mission in writing this book is in hopes of preventing others from being pushed away from God by other Christians or religious people. This book was written in real time, throughout the course of my journey, before I knew what the outcome would be. I began my walk with God as a skeptic, but when God shows up in your life there's no denying His hand at work. It is my hope that you can see the true ebbs and flows of my faith throughout the darkness of the wilderness, and experience with me, His promises, fulfilled. Most importantly, I pray it might be an encouragement for you on your walk, too.

How to Deal: *A Skeptic's Walk with Christ Through the Wilderness*

Chapter 1

My Testimony

First off, I want to let you all know that I started writing this book on a borrowed computer with two non-functioning keys on the keyboard. I had to find an H and a G somewhere on the computer to copy and paste them every time I needed one. The struggle is *real*. But it wasn't always this way.

So hi, I'm Desirée, I am nobody special. I come from humble beginnings, raised by my mother who was working her way through Nurse Practitioner school basically my entire childhood while working full time. I didn't have money growing up, I've barely gotten by most of my life. I never expected much for myself, but recently I've got a new mindset. I've found new courage that doesn't depend on my own capabilities, and I wanted to share it with you.

Growing up I never heard much about God or about Jesus. Nobody in my family went to church or even spoke about God. They weren't against religion; they just weren't involved in any of it. I remember, all my life my friends all went to church, and I was always curious about it. My first experience was when I was in elementary school. They started this program called "Religious Release" where kids were able to get on a bus and go to their church during recess.

Well, all my friends were going, so of course I wanted to go as well. It was around Christmas time, and they were teaching about Jesus being the reason for the season. The woman leading the Bible study had made a comparison of Santa with Satan, pointing out that Santa was just a ploy used by Satan in order to steal the light off of Jesus, "Notice how SANTA and SATAN have the same letters just changed around?" she said. Now, as a child who was new to the teaching of the Bible, that was scary and a lot to take in at one time. I returned home and tell my mom about it and proceed to go around telling my entire family they're going to hell; needless to say, my mother decided maybe that wasn't a good fit for me.

Years later, in about the sixth grade, my best friend was going to church camp for the summer. Throughout the year we would spend every day together, especially during the summer, so of course she told me I had to come! So, I did. It was all fun and games and we had such a great time, but when service came, I wasn't prepared. Again, as a child with no prior knowledge of the religious practices, it was a lot for me to take in at once. I was standing there in worship and suddenly someone came up to me and shoved my head down and began yelling out in this strange language I had never heard before. To say I was terrified would be an understatement. Not because it was so aggressive and unfamiliar, though it was, but because those unknown words began spilling out of *my* mouth as I sobbed uncontrollably. I had no idea what was happening, I didn't know what speaking in tongues was and although I was scared at the time, I felt equally comforted.

That comfort was quickly squashed by my friend, as we were leaving service. I was asking her about what had happened to me, and she said, "Why would you do that? You can't speak in tongues; you don't even believe in God." As if it was in my control; I didn't even know what was happening! But she didn't know any better because she was young and that was just what she had been led to believe. Regardless, I internalized that beautiful experience to be a shameful one. I didn't know it then, but looking back, that was my first introduction to the Holy Spirit, and He was just as much available to me as anyone else there, because in that moment, *I* was available.

I look back to this experience in the sixth grade and although I wasn't really sure what was happening at that time, I am convinced that because of that day, I had surely and genuinely received the Holy Spirit, and He has been with me and kept me safe throughout the crazy, and I do mean crazy, ride I have taken myself on in this here life. The decisions I had made in my young life should have killed me many, many times.

Lamentations 3:1-3 "I am one who knows what it is to be punished by God. He drove me deeper and deeper into darkness…and beat me again and again with merciless blows."

I'm writing to you because I have been through it. I know what it is to be punished by God, but it was a correction of love that I am so thankful for today.

Throughout the following years of my life, I never really believed in God, not in my head anyway. As a matter of fact, I had a big interest in conspiracy theory videos especially concerning government and, of course, religion!

I had a deep disdain for religion. I was turned off from religion at young age due to those overly religious "Christians". I had spent a lot of time studying the opposing side of religion; but now, having gone through this season in my life, there is no research I could do to convince me that this has *not* been an act of God. God steps in at the perfect time and teaches us and corrects our paths, just as our earthly parents do. Not only did I deserve it, I *needed* it.

Hebrews 12:5-6 "My child, pay attention when the Lord corrects you, and do not be discouraged when He rebukes you. Because the Lord corrects everyone He loves, and punishes everyone He accepts as a child."

First of all, the sooner you accept this, odds are, the less you'll have to endure in this season of correction which, let's face it, is a season of pain, frustration, suffering, and pure discomfort. I'll tell you now, I wish I would have accepted this much earlier in *my* journey. Oh yes, He knows what you love most, and He will use it to make you extremely uncomfortable. Sometimes He's got to break you down in order to use you for something so much greater. Not to hurt or manipulate you, but because He knows you. Some people are attacked and destroyed, but some get hit and it opens them up to their destiny and purpose.

He knew the exact moment I was ready to receive Him when He placed this man of God in my life (we'll get to him in a minute). At that time, the Lord knew I was ready to be broken down and built back up into something much greater, He knew I would have the strength, support, and guidance to endure the suffering I was about to experience and have the willingness to learn from it to become someone with a much greater purpose. He will accept and correct anybody. A-ny-body, y'all!! Drug addicts, drug dealers, prostitutes, murderers, liars, cheaters, you name it! Everybody has access to God's mercy. It does not matter what you've done, you can always turn to God.

1 Timothy 1:15-16 "Christ Jesus came into the world to save sinners. I am the worst of them, but God was merciful to me in order that Christ Jesus might show His full patience in dealing with me, the worst of sinners, as an example for all those who would later believe in Him and receive eternal life."

He came to save me. *Me.* This wasn't an elite club as I had been led to believe all these years. There were no requirements, actions, secret passwords, or dress codes to get in; I only had to believe.

I was *very* resistant to come, but looking back now, I can trace my journey back to this – although I didn't believe in God, I did come to a point of such frustration and misery in my life and in my cycle of toxic relationships where I felt there was no other option but to pray. Although I didn't believe in God in my head, as I said, I do believe He was always lying somewhere dormant in my heart. I always had the *desire* to know Him, ever since I was a kid, I just needed to hear the *truth*. I believe He is somewhere in the heart of all of us, as hard and cold as we may be, and at the right time, we'll call to Him in our time of despair, and the truth – *His* truth, will be revealed to us.

I had a history of bad relationships, terrible dating habits, all rooted in cycles of pain. Pain, anchored by more of the confusion in my life that further masqueraded itself as unbelief. However, even in confusion the Holy Spirt was still guiding me and using the negativity as a catalyst, ultimately leading me toward my purpose.

In my discovery phase, I later connected much of my negative cycles regarding men were tied to unresolved issues with my father. In life we don't get to pick our birth father, however in situations where we have childhood disappointment, if we could just connect to our Heavenly Father He will comfort and heal us, if we let Him. In life we all are like clay on the Potter's wheel, some of us let God mold us, and some appear to be finished works, a beautiful vase, only to find when we fall and break, He *uses* the broken pieces instead of throwing us away. Like a broken vase, God will come in and use our brokenness to pick us up, put us back together, and fill in the painful cracks with a love that nothing else could replace.

Like many women, I was trying to find love from a man, which was really tied to my perception of my father, yet God was guiding me the entire way. The path was not always clear, and the lies I accepted and developed about men were there because I had not exchanged my trauma from my father to God. In fact, I realized I had been projecting my issues with the father onto God, Himself. I was self-righteously dealing with so much drama in relationships. I finally broke down in my last negative relationship that I was trying to get out of, and for the first time in my life, I prayed to God:

"Lord, I know this is not the man for me, but I'm not ready to let him go. God, if you're real, let me enjoy this relationship for a little while longer without all the pain until you are ready to bring the right man into my life, and at that time, give me the strength to walk away from this one."

Now, I know that sounds like a crazy thing to ask of God, but He was crazy enough to answer me! And I know what you're thinking, "Ew, why does she think she always needs a man in her life to be happy, ehhl..." Well, that's just where I was at that point and I'm just being honest and recounting real historical events, okay? My journey was arduous, but not about the pain of the past I was carrying, or my father, but learning to find the love of God.

18

My Testimony

After moving to Florida, I had a hard time finding a good job that would pay the bills. I had graduated from college as a Licensed Practical Nurse, but I wasn't registered in the state of Florida, and I had gone to a bartending school in Nashville with a friend of mine, just for fun, but I didn't have much real bartending experience. As I was looking up my options for Florida nursing exams and bartending positions, I found that the exams were too expensive (and let's face it, I was afraid to fail) and every restaurant bartending position wanted years of experience.

Finally, I came across an ad in Craigslist looking for bartenders at a local club, no experience necessary. I was at a point in my life where I wasn't drinking or partying anymore and I was getting more serious about my future, and I didn't want to get complacent in a nightclub. But I took the job, thinking that if I just went into it as a job and not a party, I could make some quick cash and gain some experience to move on to another place of employment in a couple months.

Well, after a few weeks of turning down drinks and shots and insisting on serving sober, my manager insisted I take a shot and relax a little, which led to another, night after night, and eventually it became a routine. It got to the point that I was drunk every night and most nights I would blackout and couldn't even remember getting home, but the money was so good, I ended up staying there longer than planned and was no longer even looking for other employment options.

Just as I had feared, I had been sucked into the life. To some people, working at a club may not be a big deal at all, to others they may think it makes me less than worthy of God's love somehow, but the truth is, it doesn't matter what you did in the past to get by, you're here now – *we're* here now, and in the economy of God, your past doesn't matter, it doesn't define you. Your job doesn't matter, what you do doesn't matter; just consider, Jesus was friends with murders, thieves, adulterers, and prostitutes.

So anyway, I was at a point in my life where I was focused on myself instead of looking for a man, and then one night, this guy came up to my bar, all *fancy* dressed in a suit jacket and jeans, looking real nice, but I didn't think anything of it; I served him a drink and was on to the next. We ended up talking for a while and he asked for my number, and I politely declined, and he politely insisted. He had to catch a private flight that night and after delaying it multiple times talking to me, he ended up missing his flight just to stay a little longer and talk (and work on getting that number). Finally, he tells me he will give me his number so I can call when I'm comfortable, and just asks that I give him my number so that when I call, he'll know it's me, but he promised he won't call me first.

Well, in an attempt to get him to stop asking, I decided to give in...and give him a fake number. Typically, when I gave out a fake number, I would write down my number and just change the last number so if they ever tried to test me (learned that the hard way) I would know the number I gave them. So, I'm writing it out and I get to that last number, and I hesitate, I look up at him, and for whatever reason I decided to give him my real number; all ten digits of it.

Days go by and I don't call. One day, about a week later, I get a call – it's him. I didn't answer but I called him back later. After giving him a hard time for breaking his promise not to call, we had a nice little chat. After that he continued to stop into the club to talk and we got to know more about each other. Although he appeared to be the perfect *man:* he was mature, well put together, he was polite, friendly, and kind, he was tall, dark, and handsome, he has a daughter of whom he has full custody and No. Baby. Mama. Drama!! Girls, you know what a gem that is! He was everything I wasn't used to. But I was still very resistant to give in.

Having forgotten about my little request from the Man upstairs when I prayed that prayer, I continued to tell this guy I was not interested, and he continued to come back and try again and again. For him, it was love at first sight. He told me that God had showed me to him in a vision in a dream years ago, a woman with dark hair and "very distinct, pretty, bright green eyes". He shrugged it off at the time because he didn't know anyone who fit that description, but he said as soon as he saw me behind the bar, he knew that I was his wife.

I laughed and told him I had zero interest in getting married so, he had the wrong one. Not to mention, I'm thinking, *nice line, buddy, but I wasn't born yesterday.* I was not convinced, especially once he brought up the whole *God* thing. What did really win him over, however, is the night he asked me to dance. Not with him, not a slow dance, no no, he wanted to see *my* moves. Now I don't dance, I *have* no moves. I don't like the attention to be on me, I can't dance, I don't do "sexy" and it's just not my thing. He insisted, however and got the rest of the club to convince me to dance and they wouldn't let it go, so I caved. Now, given we were in a club I am so sure he expected some typical sexy dance, some twerkin' — *something,* but when I hit him with the robot…that really sealed the deal. This was no sexy robot either, I hit him with the full "beep bop" and all. He's been hooked ever since.

We became good friends, but as we talk, I told him how I felt about religion, and he told me about his belief in God. *Scurrrrt!* I stopped him right there and told him he can just go ahead and forget about this then, because I did not go to church, I did not believe in God, nor did I have the desire to change. You see, the thing about me is, I like my nails long, my hair long, my heels high, my eyeliner sharp, and my style *bold!* What I'm not about to do is start dressing like a church lady just to prove I can be a church lady. But beyond that, I just felt that I surely wouldn't be a good "Christian" role model for his daughter, not to the standards I felt the "church" or the Lord required, anyway!

He told me that our differences in beliefs didn't matter; in fact, he told me that he saw something different in me, and he *knew* that I would be a great role model for his daughter, and he prophesied ministry and God's call on my life. "You will see," he said with a smirk, and just left it at that.

We ended up hanging out in my very rare free time and eventually started dating. I told him how strongly I felt about not moving in together and my desire to continue working, although he would prefer it not be at the club due to the risk I was putting myself in every night. The truth is, I was uncomfortable at the substantial amount of money he made and did not want to simply waltz my way into his existing success.

The only time we were really able to see each other was for a quick breakfast in the mornings, so after I got off work at 4AM, I would drive an hour to his house and we would wake up in the morning, he would have breakfast made, we would eat and then he would take his daughter to school and I would drive an hour back home to get ready and go back to work. Eventually I decided to keep my important and most valuable things at his house since my house had become more of a storage unit since I was never there, and it would save me time having to get ready for work. Basically, we half-moved in together very quickly due to convenience and lack of free time. Exactly what I *didn't* want to do, but I figured it wasn't *really* like living together because I still had my own house, so, whatever.

Well, he convinced me to quit my job and offered to have me work for him, as he was looking for an assistant and could use some help with caring for his daughter. Now first let me say, that God works very differently with different people. Everything I said I was not going to do, happened...and I'm very stubborn, so if this wasn't God...I just don't know. So, before you go and get all righteous and theological on me, let me tell you that had I not given in to every single one of these things that seem "ungodly" or "immoral" or whatever, I *never* would have gotten to where I am today. God knows exactly what each individual needs to get to their destiny, so, it is what it is, you can't judge anyone's process. We did, however, still make the decisions, and there was plenty of sin going on, just waiting to be corrected.

Micah 6:13-14 "So I have already begun your ruin and destruction because of your sins. You will eat, but not be satisfied-in fact you will still be hungry. You will carry things off, but you will not be able to save them; anything you do save I will destroy in war. You will sow grain, but not harvest the crop."

One morning, rather than waking up and having breakfast, he had woken me up and asked me to come with him to take his daughter to school. I wasn't much of a morning person, so I said, "Ah, no thanks." He had this strange feeling that I needed to be with him, so he came back to wake me up again, insisting I go with him. He told me I didn't even have to get ready, just come and he'll take me out to breakfast and then shopping. Well, I may not be a morning person and I may cherish my sleep, but even more than all of that, I love food and I *love* shopping. So, I threw on some clothes, slipped on some shoes, and didn't even take my purse, off we went.

Our drive to the school was about an hour; we drop her off. Shortly after, we receive an alert from the security company, there was smoke detected. We brush it off as something that mistakenly tripped the alarm. Immediately after that we receive a call. It's the neighbor, telling us the house is on fire. *Now,* we're thinking, *this is odd.* Yet, we still were not convinced it was real.

We skip breakfast and shopping and speed back to the house, all the while completely convinced there had been a mistake. As we get closer, we begin to smell smoke, *Surely, it's just someone having a controlled fire,* I think to myself. We get closer and we see a very large cloud of smoke in the general direction of the home, at this point I am *still* thinking, *perhaps there's a fire close by,* still in denial that it could be true.

As we turn the corner, we see the many, many firetrucks surrounding the home. At this point I'm looking at it, and it's still not real. This beautiful, three-story beach home, up in flames. Because it was gated across the front and the beach was on the other side, the firetruck was unable to get access to the home and it took a long time for them to get water on it and extinguish it. The whole roof was caved in, and everything was destroyed. Our clothes, shoes, all our possessions, artwork, family photos, all of our Christmas gifts, my purse and all the cash I had in it, legal documents, computers – everything.

*Job 20:26 "Everything they have saved is destroyed; a fire not lit by
human hands burns them and all their family."
Joel 1:16 "We look on helpless as our crops are destroyed."*

Ooh…felt that. There was nothing we could do, we sat in the car and watched helplessly as the house was up in flames. I should have died that morning; and had he not heard and been obedient in listening to God, I would have. It was never about breakfast or shopping or spending time together, the Holy Spirit was urging him to get me up and out of that house. The fire marshal actually told us that had anyone been in the home they would never have been able to survive it. Our bedroom where I would have been sleeping was on the third floor, so I couldn't have jumped. The windows were hurricane impact glass, and the roof was Spanish tiled, so the home was literally an insulated inferno with no place for the heat to escape. I would have been cooked.

We went to visit the remains days after, and I took photos of the bed where I would have ordinarily been sleeping on any other morning – where I *should* have been sleeping *that* morning. We looked through the ash to see what we could recover. My boyfriend pried open the charred dresser that had been welded completely shut by fire, I took a photo of him as he was looking through the charred remains. What I didn't realize at that time is in that photo, he was pulling out from underneath a towel, which seemed to perfectly preserve, his Bible, perfect, uncharred, and didn't so much as *smell* of smoke. Looking back now, it was the perfect symbol of the journey we were about to embark on. And this was just the beginning.

Malachi 2:2 "You must honor Me by what you do. If you will not listen to what I say, then I will bring a curse on you. I will put a curse on the things you receive for your support. In fact, I have already put a curse on them, because you do not take My command seriously."

Now that we have survived, we are being tested and purified. His business deals were falling apart, partners refuse to pay what they owe, clients drop out of deals; we had no money coming in and insurance is slowly addressing liability. Look, you guys, as miserable as it seems, this is all part of God's process!

My Testimony

Zechariah 13:7-9 "I will attack My people and throughout the land two-thirds of the people will die. And I will test the third that survives and will purify them as silver is purified by fire. I will test them as gold is tested. Then they will pray to Me, and I will answer them. I will tell them that they are My people, and they will confess that I am their God."

Apparently, we were the third that survived in this scenario, but I wasn't ready to pray just yet. I wish I would have though, because if I thought I had been through devastation at that point, y'all, I had no idea. The real devastation was right around the corner. Now comes the testing.

We had no idea where we were going to go or ultimately end up landing, so we made the choice to start homeschooling. We ultimately moved and things were looking good for us; we had some savings, so over time we were able to replace some things we had lost in the fire. We, of course, had to replace kitchen stuff, food, furniture, hair stuff, makeup, nail stuff, all the little things you don't think of that really begin to add up. We went shopping, got new clothes, shoes, and we were eating good every night. We frequented a sushi restaurant so often we became friends with our waitresses. Every time we came in, they would all come meet us at the door with hugs, greet us by name, people thought we were celebrities in there! One waitress in particular, became good friends with us. She would bring us full trays of complementary desserts, gold dusted chocolates, we got, literally, the gold star treatment.

It got to the point that we got tired of eating so much sushi, but we loved our little fam there, so we stopped in to say hi before going out to grab dinner somewhere else. Our waitress said, "Oh, what are you going to have?" we told her we were going to find some steak and lobster somewhere. She said, "If you want to stay, I will get you steak from next door and they have lobster across the street, I'll put it together and plate it for you and bring it here." After we agreed, it started raining and she literally ran across the street in the rain for us to bring us a special order.

One day she brought me some of her homemade lobster fried rice to try and it was *so good*, she knew it was my favorite so every time we gave her a heads up that we were coming in she would cook lobster fried rice for me and bring it in along with her homemade (super-hot) hot sauce. Even the people at the hibachi restaurant knew us by name. We were like local celebrities, living large; at this point, we thought we were in the clear. We were so spoiled, we couldn't want for anything, but yet, something was always missing.

My Testimony

Revelation 3:17 "You say, 'I am rich and well off; I have all I need. But you do not know how miserable and pitiful you are! You are poor, naked, and blind."

This was so true! I had no idea how miserable I was until I lost everything I had. The Lord was trying to reach us. As a Christian man of God, my boyfriend knew it, too. I remember he had suggested one day out of the blue, that we should serve at a shelter or get involved at a church, something to give back. But that was as far as that thought went, we never actually acted on it. I see, now, that had we just been obedient the first time He was calling us, we may not have had to suffer *as* much.

Eventually we begin to get low on our savings and still have no income coming in. As the stress begins to set in, I begin putting pressure on my boyfriend to do something. All I ever saw him doing was going off with his Bible to pray, as he urged me that we are to wait upon the Lord. One day I had just had enough, and I busted into the room where he was praying and said, "Can you just *do something!!* Like *do* SOMETHING!*"* He was sitting there with his Bible in his hand and said, "I am. This instruction is from the Lord and doing this will get us so much farther than if I just go out and try to handle it myself."

Hosea 5:15 "I will abandon My people until they have suffered enough for their sins and come looking for Me. Perhaps in their suffering they will try to find Me."

Well, apparently, he got the memo. I, however, was still not there yet. Needless to say, I didn't take to that response very well. As if things couldn't get any worse, one day the Lord tells him, like when God spoke to Abraham, "Go, leave everything behind and go." After all the money spent replacing what we had lost, he expected us to just, leave it all and go away? Where? Why?? I suppose this scripture explains it…

Proverbs 28:14 "Always obey the Lord and you will be happy. If you are stubborn, you will be ruined."

The Lord told him to leave everything behind by faith, as what I can only assume to be a true show of obedience to His voice and instruction, as the scriptures stated, but in no kind of way at that time was I *ever* going to let that happen (if only I knew that scripture then like I know it now). We left our house we were renting, as instructed, and we were on traveling assignments, staying in hotels trying to find God's direction, mind you, we are already low on our savings.

My Testimony

I reached out to the realtor we had been working with and asked him to pack up our belongings and put them in storage for us and we would send him the keys and money for the movers, the storage, and for him. He agrees, gets it packed up, sets up automatic payments for the storage and finally, I can breathe a little. But I still need answers.

As funds continue to dwindle down, my boyfriend meets up with a longtime friend who he financially blessed years ago and wanted to return the favor. He invites us to stay with him for a while and we do. He has a spare bedroom for the three of us, his daughter, him, and I, and we make it work.

One day, his girlfriend tells him she doesn't feel like she can relax around the house with guests, and she would like us to go. Of course, we don't want to impose, so we leave. We end up at another hotel and at this point we had shut off our phone because we couldn't afford the expense. As if things were not already headed in the wrong direction, our car got towed and we couldn't get it out due to the expense, so we lost it.

Finally, when we don't know how we'll pay for our next night at the hotel, my boyfriend turns to me and says, "I know this isn't what you signed up for. I don't blame you if you want to leave. I can gather some money from a couple business partners who are past due on payment, I'll give it all to you and help you get to wherever you need to go." It wasn't until this point that I had ever truly felt a love so deep and unconditional for anyone before, suddenly our circumstances didn't matter. I looked him in his eyes and told him with all confidence, "I'm not going anywhere. We'll get through this." It was at that point that we both knew without a doubt, we'd make it – through this, through life, we could get through anything together, because we had each other through the best and the absolute worst of times.

At this point, looking back I know this was not me. "Me" would always leave a situation any time I was uncomfortable. "Me" would break up with a guy and move across the country that same night. "Me" does not stick through the uncomfortable times willingly. This was definitely an act of God.

He reaches out to another friend who allows us to stay with him. He comes to pick us up and the three of us, again, share the spare bedroom. Once again, *his* girlfriend begins to feel like she is unable to be the "woman of the house" so we agree to leave the house for a few hours during the day so they can be alone. We didn't have a car though so we had to spend money we didn't have on some jackets so we could go walk around a walking path outside in the cold for hours, every day. We did whatever we could to not be an imposition.

One night she apparently had enough, we could hear them arguing in the other room and he ended up coming into our room around 2AM, apologizing that his girlfriend wanted us to leave. They literally expected us to wake up our 11-year-old, get her out of bed and in the middle of the night, with nowhere to go. After thinking it over he let us stay that night. The next day we all sat down to talk. She said she wanted us to leave because, she said, "I don't know you".

Hebrews 13:2 "Remember to welcome strangers in your homes. There were some who did that and welcomed angels without knowing it."

We understood, beyond that, she had been trying to start a family and begin the next stage of her life and there was a lot of pressure and frustration on her already with life not going as planned. I didn't blame her; I don't blame them – any of them. We walked on eggshells to be respectful and try to stay out of the way the best we could, we bought food and cooked for everyone, we cleaned up after ourselves as well as general cleaning around the house. We stayed in our room as often as we possibly could to stay out of the way, but nothing was ever good enough.

It literally *had* to be the Lord turning them against us because it just didn't make sense. Who treats people that way? I understand it being an imposition, but for goodness' sake we lost our home, all our money and had a child with us. And these were not bad people, the man was absolutely one of the sweetest guys you'd ever meet, and his girlfriend was not a bad person either! This was a spiritual move, and I know it!

Zechariah 8:10-12 "Before that time — no one was safe from enemies. I turned people against each other. But now I am treating the survivors — differently. They will plant their crops in peace. Their vines will bear grapes, the earth will produce crops, and there will be plenty of rain. I will give <u>all</u> these blessings to the people — who survive."

Y'all, I have never experienced being treated this way ever for any reason. Somewhere in the following days, I finally broke; I mean really, really broke. Calmly and very sternly I told my boyfriend he had to find a vehicle to borrow so we can go to the storage unit, which was out of town. Now, typically when I'm emotionally amped up like that, he won't ask questions, he'll just find a way to get me what I need or what I'm asking for.

This time he asked why. Perhaps it was my creepy calmness that tipped him off. I told him I just needed to get there, and again he asked, why? At that moment I snapped and told him softly, "Because I need to get my ****ing gun...so I can finally just bl*w my ****ING...FACE OFF!!" As the words finally escaped my mouth, I broke out sobbing for the first time since the fire sent us into this hell spiral we've been in. I was so frustrated, embarrassed, humiliated, and broken down, I didn't know what else to do. Not a single ounce of it was seeking attention, I fully meant what I said. I just wanted to end it, and had he just taken me to the storage unit that day, I would have. I couldn't physically take it anymore. But there was a purpose for it all.

In every rejection was God's hand moving us, pushing us to where He needed us to be. Leaving the first home we were at pushed us to the second, which brought us to the city where we currently live to this day. It is the city where we ultimately found our church and I got baptized. It is the place that changed everything for me, for us. It's the place God intended for us to be all along.

Acts 17:26-27 "[God] Himself fixed beforehand the exact times and the limits of the places where they would live. He did this so that they would look for Him, and perhaps find Him as they felt around for Him."

All the devastation had brought us here. After we sat down and talked things out with them that next day, she agreed to allow us to stay until we could find a place to move. This was right before Christmas, so when Christmas came around, he invited us to watch his friend's daughter's piano recital with him, and we agreed to go.

Afterward, as we're riding in the car, he asked if we'd like to go to his church's Christmas program. I instantly began sweating. My boyfriend says, "Sure, when is it?" meanwhile, I'm in the back seat trying to figure out in my head how I'm going to get us out of going. He says, "It's about to start, we can head over right now!" *Nooooooo!!* I thought, *There's no escape, I'm just going to show up, walk through those doors and BURST into flames. Wonderful.* I had always felt this way because in my experience with "the church" I tend to not be accepted. I don't dress like them, I don't talk like them, I don't act like them, I don't walk like them. I was out of my element, the fear was setting in.

Alas, we make it through the doors, and I do not, in fact, combust. In fact, I am greeted by a woman who hugs me the warmest, most genuine hug I have *ever* received from a stranger. I was not a hugger, myself, but it was so refreshing, so unexpected. It really caught me by surprise.

Anyway, we find our seats, wayyy in the back, watch the cute little program, and afterward, the pastor preaches a short message. Though it was short, it had a way of addressing and correcting so many misconceptions I had about who God is and how He feels about me, about everyone. My boyfriend turned to me and said, "I have been to a lot of churches, I have heard a lot of preaching, this place is heavily anointed." I didn't know what that meant at the time, but I felt it as well. This church was like nothing I ever expected it to be. I knew I just had to be there, we had to go back. We were hungry!

Amos 8:11 "The time is coming when I will send famine on the land. People will be hungry, but not for bread; they will be thirsty, but not for water. They will hunger and thirst for a message from the Lord."

From that day forward we did whatever it took to borrow a car every Sunday and make it to service; we never missed a single one. One service the pastor had an altar call. I didn't know what the heck that was, I just saw my boyfriend slide past me without saying a word, left his backpack he carried everywhere with everything important we owned in it, and began walking up to the stage. I had no clue what was going on. *Do I stay here? Do I follow? Do I leave the bag or take it with me?* Eventually I picked up the bag and followed behind him.

The pastor led us in a prayer and told us to go to the chapel for a gift and prayer. We follow the crowd into the chapel, receive prayer and they give us a Bible. We took it home and I never thought about it again. I had never read the Bible before, the only experience I had with the Bible was opening drawers in hotel rooms and seeing it in there. That's it. Never opened one – nothing.

One day I was sitting around, and it caught my eye. I decided to open it up and see what it was about. I had no idea where to start, so I just opened it up. I found myself in the book of Job. I could so relate to the sudden loss and tragic series of events Job was going though that I got completely sucked in. I picked up that Bible and I couldn't put it down. I was inspired by the way God turned Job's whole situation around; I took it as instruction for my own mess I was in.

Finally, 4AM rolls around, and I'm still reading, I had read through the entire New Testament, highlighting, taking notes, and writing down questions. Finally, my boyfriend says, "Hunny, it'll still be there tomorrow, you can go to bed now." I was so invested; the stories were so good! So inspiring! I was so encouraged and uplifted!

My Testimony

Matthew 4:4 "But Jesus answered, 'The scripture says, 'Human beings cannot live on bread alone, but need every Word that God speaks.'"

Through everything we've been through, we have never been without food. We may have bought groceries with loose cupholder change a time or two; God allowed us to struggle, but never starve. But we did have a hunger for Jesus, and now I truly understand the meaning of the bread of life.

2 Corinthians 4:8-9 "We are often troubled, but not crushed; sometimes in doubt, but never in despair; there are many enemies, but we are never without a friend; and though badly hurt at times, we are not destroyed."

The events in my life were painful, they hurt – bad; but I was never destroyed. In fact, had I not turned to the Bible at this time, I am convinced that I would have eventually found a way to "end it". The book of Job gave me hope – it saved my life.

Now, as we search for a place to live, we realize we have nowhere near the money we need for a deposit, and money is still not coming in, so my boyfriend reaches out to an old business partner, we borrow a car to meet with him, he offers a significant check, but the Lord says, "No" so he walks away from something that could have literally changed everything for us in an instant. But greater than our faith in the money and what we could do with it, we (or he) fully trusted God. When the Lord came to my boyfriend in a vision allowing him to choose life's next direction, God told him, "There's a fork in the road, you can go this way and do things your way, self-righteously, and fall back on your education, skillset, and abilities, but My hand will not be upon you. Or you can go My way, listen, and obey Me, and I will bless you, but you won't know what it's going to look like."

Micah 4:2 "He will teach us what He wants us to do; we will walk in the paths He has chosen."

So, after driving all that way, he rejects the offer, we drive back with nothing, and the next day he goes out humbly, walking place to place to find a job. Since he has been self-employed for the past eighteen years, and was well overqualified for any of these jobs, people were reluctant to hire him. Finally, he convinces an underpaying local company to hire him, I guess at the time something was better than nothing, little did we know it would be the very thing to connect us to our greatest blessing.

Zechariah 4:10 "Do not despise these small beginnings, for the Lord rejoices to see the work begin."
Ecclesiastes 9:11 "The wise do not always earn a living, intelligent people do not always get rich, and capable people do not always rise to

*high positions. Bad luck happens to everyone. You never know when
your time is coming."*

Holy cannoli, isn't that the TRUTH! But he worked
with what he could get. He walked to work and back about a
mile both ways in the scorching Florida sun and in the rain.
He never missed a day, never showed up late, and never took
a vacation. We didn't know why in the *world* the Lord would
have him reject that check just to work for someone else and
be underpaid, but my boyfriend, fully capable of elevating and
asserting himself, knew that it was not about being self-
righteous, but fully trusted that God was in control and
would work *all* things out for our good.

*Romans 8:28 "And we know that God causes everything to work
together for the good of those who love God and are called according to
His purpose for them." NLT*

Eventually, we thought we had enough for a deposit
on an apartment, but first we'd need a car. We didn't have
much to spend, but fortunately, the guy we were staying with
had a friend who owned a used car "buy here pay here" lot,
so we went to see what he might be willing to offer us. We
met him at his house after driving by the lot; he didn't have a
lot to choose from, but we were in no position to be picky.
As we were about to leave to go back to the lot with him, we

saw this beautiful white convertible Mercedes his wife had been driving, parked in his garage. He said they had just got it in, and his wife was driving it until it sold, though she didn't really want to sell it. But he is a businessman after all, so when he saw my eyes light up, he asked if we were interested.

Um, yes! God's favor must have showed up because the next events just do not make sense. *He* asked *us* how much we could put down on it, and as ridiculous and silly as it seemed to even suggest, my boyfriend said, "fifty dollars." He reached out his hand, "You got a deal," he said, "fifty dollars down and two-hundred dollars a month, can you do that?" We took the deal, no credit check, no interest, and he let us have it for five-thousand dollars. That was such a blessing that we never could have made happen without God.

Now was time to find an apartment. I was able to find a nice little studio condo on the beach. It would be tight living for the three of us, but it had a beautiful view and was more affordable than most other units in the area, and we just needed something…and *fast*. I showed up to look at the unit, signed the paperwork and gave them the deposit that same day. In the meantime, the people we were staying with had to move out of their apartment because the owner was selling it, so we all had a deadline to be out of there, in a week. As the moveout date is approaching and we are preparing to move, I get a call from the owners of our new place. They had gone to the unit to get everything cleaned and ready for move in when they found bedbugs. They said unfortunately they would have to get the exterminators to come before we could move in which wouldn't be until *after* we had to move out, leaving us no place to stay in the meantime.

Just when things were starting to look up, everything was starting to fall apart. I got in the shower to escape everyone and just lost it. I was sobbing uncontrollably into the water, praying, and pleading with God to lead us to the right place and not allow us to end up on the street. We were *days away* from being *literally* homeless under a bridge. How could we have fallen so far? How do we go from a solid, secure life to...*this?* We didn't have enough time to find a place, look at the unit, pay for and fill out the application, wait to get approved...there was no time! I was so broken down and desperate. I *needed* a move of God. I could not make this happen without Him!

I found an apartment that was as cheap as I could possibly find, it was a one-bedroom apartment for $899 a month, fully furnished, with all utilities included. I showed up to look at the unit, paid for the background check and application, filled it out and left it there that day. When they contacted me back, they said I was approved, however they needed first and last month's rent plus an additional security deposit. We had just enough saved so we agreed to take it. We asked if we could move in that next day. They said yes, but the rent for the remainder of the month would be prorated and we just couldn't afford it, however, we did need to get in a few days early because we needed time to move in, and our very next paycheck gave us, to the dollar, exactly what we needed to move in when we needed to. To. The. Dollar.

Job 37:4 "Seek your happiness in the Lord, and He will give you your hearts desire. Give yourself to the Lord; trust in Him and He will help you"

At this point, there was nothing I wanted more than to be approved for this little one-bedroom apartment; that was the extent my imagination could think to ask or believe God for at that time, it was all I desperately wanted – to not end up on the street. I had no choice but to trust Him to make a way, there was just literally no time. But He led us to that place. He got us there safely, despite all my stressing. I never ended up on the street, even though it was a *suuuper* close call.

Deuteronomy 1:29 But I told you, "Don't be afraid of those people. The Lord your God will lead you, and He will fight for you, just as you saw

Him do in Egypt and in the desert. You saw how He brought you safely all the way to this place, just as a father would carry his son." But in spite of what I said, you still would not trust the Lord, even though He always went ahead of you to find a place for you to camp.

I tried, after this, I did. I wanted to trust the Lord. We were finally independent again, we had a car, a job, a place to live, but the hell spiral was far from over.

Now that we had got settled and got a phone temporarily, we reached out to our realtor friend who had our belongings in storage. *Finally,* I thought, *I can go pick up what's left of my belongings, and I can begin to feel normal again.* I called and was immediately met with bad news. He thought he had set up the payments to be automatic, however, it somehow wasn't being taken out, and therefore not being paid for months, and they sold our unit and everything we owned. Literally, everything.

Ruth 1:21 "When I left here, I had plenty, but the Lord has brought me back without a thing."

So, I guess when the Lord told us to leave and leave it all behind, He must have really meant it…as hard as I tried to work my way around it and hold on, He will get what He wants in the end. It wasn't like I was just trying to be

47

rebellious against what He told us to do, I guess in my mind at that time it just didn't make sense. Why would God *want* us to walk away from all our stuff and have nothing? That's just weird. For what purpose, like – I have questions!

Obadiah 1:5-6 "But your enemies have wiped you out completely. Descendants of Esau, your treasures have been looted. Your allies have deceived you; they have driven you from your country. – Those friends who ate with you have laid a trap for you."

Why? This is someone we considered a friend; did he rip us off? I don't know…it's possible. It's actually very likely. But again, I don't blame him if he did, God told us to let it all go, leave it, and we didn't listen; well, half listened. I may never fully understand why God would want us to give up everything we have worked for, but I guess we wouldn't be the first…Abraham, Joseph, and Jonah to name a few.

Job 18-19 "They have to give up all they have worked for; they will have no chance to enjoy their wealth."

We literally worked so hard for what we had and then again to replace what was lost in the fire and we couldn't even enjoy it! We spent all that money to replace things we lost just to leave it all behind. I never understood why. Why would God let us spend all that money to replace things just to *ask* us to leave it and then *force* us to leave it by having it taken from us?

Ecclesiastes 6:7&9 "We do all our work just to get something to eat, but we never have enough. — It is better to be satisfied with what you have than to be always wanting something else."

I understand now that the experience of giving up everything we had and living with nothing, has taught us more than listening to a life coach, TED talk, sermon, or even reading a scripture ever could…it has taught us to be satisfied with what we have, whether it's a lot or a little. Now when things go wrong, I have a perspective of just how bad things could be, and the everyday irritants don't seem quite as bad. When I had everything and lost a little, I'd be irate. Now that I have a little something, if I lose some, I'm just thankful I haven't lost it all.

In the appearance of punishment, I have learned to accept God's correction gladly, whether I understand it or not, and remain joyful through the process. That's the thing, if you're going to receive correction, it's going to come whether you like it or not, so you might as well be at peace with it and say, God, I trust You.

2 Corinthians 6:9-10 "Although punished, we are not killed; although saddened, we are always glad; we seem poor, but we make many people rich; we seem to have nothing, yet we really possess everything."

It's beginning to make some sense now. He was building our character and showing us that there is more to life than having possessions. That we can be punished and poor but still have joy. Joy is a state of being, not merely an emotion based on circumstances. We can choose to *be* joyful no matter what's going on. Joy is just as accessible in the midst of lack, pain, and suffering as it is in abundance. We can trust Him through the pain. He is good regardless of what it looks like.

2 Corinthians 7:4 "I am so sure of you; I take such pride in you! In all our troubles I am still full of courage; I am running over with joy."
2 Corinthians 7:10 "For the sadness that is used by God brings a change of heart that leads to salvation — and there is no regret in that!"

It took all of this devastation for me to see God. It led to my salvation. Nothing less than exactly what I went through could have got me to the relationship I have with God today. I had to know Him for myself. I had to fall all the way to the bottom to let Him pick me back up and dust me off when I was broken and couldn't do it myself. I can speak to others now, about who God is, from a very real and personal place.

Ecclesiastes 7:3 "Sorrow is better than laughter; it may sadden your face, but it sharpens your understanding."

Had I not hit rock bottom, I never would have looked up and searched for Him. Never. I would have simply continued on with my selfish, resentful life. I have been on both sides; I have had more than enough, and I have had nothing more than the clothes on my body, and I don't resent a minute of it. I see purpose in every miserable step of it. But I only see that perspective because I *remained* faithful to God throughout the process, and I know He's not done yet, but in the meantime, I am content.

Philippians 4:11-13 "I am not saying this because I feel neglected, for I have learned to be satisfied with what I have. I know what it is to be in need and what it is to have more than enough. I have learned this secret, so that anywhere, at any time, I am content, whether I am full or hungry, whether I have too much or too little. I have strength to face all conditions by the power that Christ gives me."

As I continue through this journey the Lord has me on, I trust in Him. When things go wrong, even terribly, terribly wrong, I am so at peace with it all, because I know it could be worse, and even if it was worse, God is with me; He is in control. I trust the process, it's never as bad as it seems. Life is about more than how I feel about it. I have the strength in the Lord to endure all things. What's gone is gone, oh well, I push forward. It won't break me, and even if it is unto death, I still win, because to die on earth is to be with the Lord, and there is no greater victory. So, what really is there to fear?

Hebrews 11:15-16 "They did not keep thinking about the country they had left; if they had, they would have had the chance to return. Instead, it was a better country they longed for, the Heavenly country."

There were times I looked back and thought about returning to the life I had before, but I realize no suffering can last forever unless you let it. At least at the end of *this* path, I have a promise to claim. So instead, I give it to God, trust in Him and know that He will bring me into a tremendous glory far greater than the trouble I endured.

2 Corinthians 4:17 "And this small and temporary trouble we suffer will bring us a tremendous and eternal glory, much greater than the trouble."

So now we have gained all this experience and wisdom that gave us such a great testimony we were so eager to share. We were so thirsty to serve God, but there seemed to be no opportunity. We were expecting to bust through those doors and dive straight into full-time ministry, sharing our firsthand experience of God's goodness and provision! We thought we were so ready! (Meanwhile, we still weren't even married.) Well, we continued to grow and mature in our faith and continued to look for another door to kick in. Didn't happen. Everything we were asking God for and believing for was just not happening!

Even though we weren't seeing any opportunity for "full-time" ministry, God used us mightily even in our weakness; we demonstrated the greater works of Jesus wherever we went and participated in miracles, signs, and wonders. Many nights tired after long day of work and school, we served God's people.

We served as mentors in our church's orphans ministry, helping teens who were aging out of foster care, which was perhaps the biggest, unexpected blessing of all my life. We ministered to a fellow believer's two-year-old child that had been diagnosed with stage four cancer, praying, laying hands-on, prophesying over his life, and witnessing a miracle of full healing. We attended countless ministry conferences where we came as spectators, only to be directly prophesied over about how the Lord was abundantly expanding our ministry, yet still, no open door.

We ended up going to a conference where Smith Wigglesworth's great granddaughter, Lilian DeFin was speaking, and she called us out to speak to us. She asked, "What is your relationship to each other?" I said, "We're…dating." Now, typically when a couple is putting off getting married, you would assume it's the man dragging his feet, but she looked directly at me and said, "Why are you keeping him waiting?" I proceeded to give her my list of excuses, "Well, we had a house fire and lost all our money, we haven't had a chance and we just want to wait unti-" she interrupted me right there, "No," she said, "*Why* are you keeping him waiting? The blessings you've been asking for that God wants to give you, are being held up in this." as she points back and forth between the two of us. Now, that wasn't the first time we had been told that we need to get married and be under God's blessing, but this time just hit different.

We left that conference and I said, "Okay Lord, if this is what You want, we'll do it." Not that I didn't want to be married to my boyfriend, he's great; it's just that I had never wanted to get married at all, let alone in the middle of all this mess. I mean, I couldn't even believe I had lasted *this* long.

54

But to sign up for a lifetime with no guarantee of things getting any better? Whoa buddy! But that's faith, right? I mean, we've already experienced better and worse, richer and poorer, sickness and health, what's left to test? I think we've got this! I think we'll do okay.

So, I knew that if we were going to do this, it *had* to be done by our pastor, who really was the vessel that got me to understand the truth and genuine goodness of God, he baptized us, and he just played such a big role in our spiritual lives. The only problem was, he wasn't really doing weddings anymore. Well, I figured if it was truly what God wanted, He would make a way, because I wasn't going to do it without my pastor.

One day after service, pastor was hanging out at the altar and talking to people not far from us, so as my boyfriend is talking to someone else, I'm standing next to him thinking, *you better go ask and find out.* I didn't even tell my boyfriend where I was going or what I was doing.

Now of all days, this happens to be the one day I'm wearing flat shoes, mind you, my boyfriend is 6'6" so I am used to some height, but my 5'6"-self felt about 4'3" when I approached pastor alone and flat to the ground. He greeted me and I said, "Um, I was wondering if, um, if we were to get married, do you think you could, um, of-officiate our wedding?" I can't tell you why I was so painfully timid, maybe because I don't like asking things of people, perhaps because I had already heard that he doesn't do weddings anymore and it felt out-of-line, I don't know. But he smiled, grabbed my face in both hands and said, "If I'm on this planet and I'm around, I wouldn't miss it."

Holyyyy moley. Everyone I knew on staff at the church was shocked like we just got the golden ticket, not because pastor is too good for his people or anything, he's literally the kindest human, but he is *so* busy constantly traveling during the week and preaching everywhere, nobody could believe he could find the time.

Well, I guess the Lord answered. Now to figure out how to afford a wedding in record time. Turns out that was of no concern either, the church staff pulled together and helped us fill in the gaps of whatever we were missing and fortunately, our wedding date happened to be during the church's fast so there was no need to have food, though we did have small snacks just in case. I wasn't even going to get a dress, but I ended up having my mom order me one off Amazon…I made my own decorations and bouquet from Dollar Tree items, and we made it work.

We got married, and after all the expenses we had a single hundred-dollar bill to our name on the day of our wedding. I remember because I took it out to give to my mom to pay her back for ordering my wedding dress. She refused to take it (thank God, because it was all we had, but I didn't let her know that).

Now that we're married, *surely,* the Lord is going to *throw* us into full-time ministry! Nope. So, back to work he goes. I still couldn't understand why he had to be at an underpaid job when he was qualified for more, until one day while he was at work, he met a Woman of God who saw ministry in him and the call on his life. She approached him and prophesied saying he had healing in his hands, a calling on his life, and told him God has abundance for him. She went inside her purse and got her checkbook and offered to pay for his choice of university.

Now, not only did he tell her he could never accept such an offer, but we didn't even know how he was going to find the *time* to go to school. Not to mention, he already had earned multiple undergraduate and post-graduate degrees, but she absolutely insisted that the Lord told her to do it and she wouldn't disobey Him, so she sent him to school.

He made the time, got accepted, fast tracked with dual enrollment for a Master's Degree in Theology and PhD in Clinical Psychology and Pastoral Counseling. At that point it finally began making sense why the Lord had him at this job. He gets the glory when it's His plan and His provision, and you can't possibly doubt His provision when it comes from a stranger who has no idea who you are.

Ok so *now* we're doin' things! We're super qualified now, you can't tell us nothing! We look around yet again for that door; at this point we expect that thing to be already sitting wide open. Um, no. Ok so, now I'm confused! What is it really going to take? I get it, I'm literally just stuck here for life. A broke chick with a whole family of three in a one bedroom one bathroom apartment with black mold in the corners. Awesome. Thanks God, I thought we were cool. Where are You Bro?? And *whyyy* will nobody take us seriously? Why is nobody listening?!

Ecclesiastes 9:15-16 "Someone lived there who was poor, but so clever that he could have saved the town. But no one thought about him. I have always said that wisdom is better than strength, but no one thinks of the poor as wise or pays any attention to what they say."

For *reallllll*. But God was hiding us in the little places of life, preparing and testing us for the greater things to come. I will never in all my life, as old or as wealthy as I may ever become, ever forget the day my husband and I went into the body shop where our totaled vehicle had been repaired, and the shop owner refused to give us an itemized receipt for the six thousand dollars' worth of work we were paying for.

My husband explained that we need it for our security in the transaction and our files and that as a business owner…(the owner of the shop cuts him off) "How are *you* going to tell me how to run *my* &*$# business?" he screamed. Now, my husband could have tongue lashed him, his vernacular is superb, and in business he is so tactical that he could cut you with words and you would not even know you were bleeding, but in this situation, he remained calm, cool, and collected. It still broke my entire literal heart and shattered my soul, to see my husband, as intelligent and as educated and as kind and generous as he is, sit there, stunned, non-reactive to the ignorant insults that he could defend up and down and put this guy down in every way.

My husband chose to take the high road, due to spiritual maturity and understanding the battle is not ours it is the Lord's. He paid the guy the money and accepted a general receipt (not itemized), continued the transaction with kindness, and left politely. This experience showed me that you can *never* know someone else's potential or worth based on their job, position or where you see them or perceive them to be in life. You *never* know what someone's potential is.

Still, I wonder, how could someone have accomplished all that my husband has, and be seen this way? Looked down upon through all his wisdom and expertise, through all the education and credentials; and still be seen as nothing more than an ignorant employee. Well, they did it to Jesus, so we are in good company. Some days it felt as if fellow believers viewed us in the same way, but what we came to realize is that He called us, and *He* equips us. It is not by power and not by might but by Him...our calling is equally as important as His timing. If you birth too soon you might abort. You have to be able to handle the spotlight with character or you will "burn".

People have been prophesying to us for years that our breakthrough will not come through who we are, what we've done, what we know or who we know. It will have nothing to do with us so that God will get all the glory; but how does someone just rest in that? We're adamant on making a way for ourselves, finding our lane, our door, anything. I think that's just human nature; it's what the world teaches us, anyway. What can *we* do?! Show me Lord, just lead me and I'll go! I am worn out from the suffering and insults. I'm sick of being overlooked. Am I missing it? (Of course, I wasn't, He already told us our breakthrough wouldn't come by way of us in any way, I just couldn't wrap my mind around that.)

My frustration and faith ebbed and flowed; I had my days. One day I got particularly frustrated and asked my husband, "Why now that I have this relationship with God, do we have all this mess and destruction? I have never had this much chaos in all my life, is this what being a Christian is about? Because I think maybe I'll pass." He explained to me that the enemy wasn't attacking me this way before, because I wasn't a threat to his kingdom (of this world). Now that I am on fire for God and eager to share my experiences and testimony of God's goodness with people, the enemy is trying to block it, discourage me and convince me to quit and turn back.

Hebrews 10:32-39 "Remember how it was with you in the past. In those days, after God's light had shown on you, you suffered many things, yet were not defeated by the struggle. You were at times publicly insulted and mistreated, and at other times you were ready to join those who were being treated in this way. You shared the sufferings of prisoners, and when all your belongings were seized, you endured your loss gladly, because you knew that you still possessed something much better, which would last forever. Do not lose your courage, then, because it brings with it a great reward. You need to be patient, in order to do the will of God and receive what He promises. For, as the scripture says, 'Just a little while longer, and he who is coming will come; he will not delay. My righteous people, however, will believe and live; but if any of them turns back, I will not be pleased with them.' We are not people who turn back and are lost. Instead, we have faith and are saved."

This scripture explains it perfectly. I like to think I am one who will believe and live, that I will not turn back but will have faith and be saved; but realistically, from where I'm sitting, it's *so hard!* My mind keeps wanting me to say, forget this, turn back, and give up the faith life, but I know deep down I would be lost, as I was before.

Surely it is a great thought to rest in – that I can basically just sit back and chill until the Lord sends some stranger along my way to bless us in a way that will turn this all around; but that just doesn't happen for me. As someone who spent her entire young adulthood being shamed and resented for asking my dad for "too much", or, really just expecting things he was responsible to provide and even said he would provide and being let down, my expectations for receiving are literally nonexistent.

I mean, my entire life, outside of my mom and now my husband, nobody ever *gave* me anything, and even if someone were to offer, I would be super uncomfortable to receive it. I'm the type of person that always wants to do the most for people so that just in case they ever offer me something I don't feel like a charity case; I never want a handout. And if I give the world to someone and they never give anything back, even better! But there is a difference between a handout and a blessing or a promise from God, and if we become too prideful to receive from Him *through* the hands of somebody else, then we only have ourselves to blame for lack of progress.

It's like that story where the guy was drowning and praying to God to come save him, meanwhile a boat comes by and offers to save him and he sends it away saying, "No thanks, I'll wait on God." Then when he drowns and meets God in Heaven, he asks Him why He never showed up to save him, the Lord says, "What do you mean, I sent you a boat!" Don't expect God to show up as an orb and hand deliver your blessing; He uses people, accept His blessing!

Laminations 3:21 "Yet hope returns when I remember this one thing: the Lord's unfailing love and mercy still continue, fresh as the morning, as sure as the sunrise. The Lord is all I have, and so in Him I put my hope."

There is one thing I try to hold tightly to, and that is that this season cannot last forever. I trust in God's Word and in the meantime, hard as it may be, I need to hold on to courage, be patient and just prepare by faith for His reward! I have no other choice! He is my only hope.

For the past five years my husband has been working relentlessly without a break, extra hours, no vacations, no sick days, and serving God's people, all while completing a dual-enrolled Master's and PhD, just trying to get ahead and although we've been blessed, there is no way it will ever get us where He has promised us. He could have taken any corporate job he wanted or started another business, he is more than qualified, yet he chose to humble himself and let God elevate him, ensuring God gets all the glory! He had a call of God on his life, and for years he was running from it, yet what he was running from he ran right into, and he realized it. Through the trauma of loss, he did not complain, he did not try to elevate himself in his own abilities, he fully submitted to God.

Ecclesiastes 5:18-19 "Here is what I have found out: the best thing we can do is eat and drink and enjoy what we have worked for during the short life that God has given us; this is our fate. If God gives us wealth and property and lets us enjoy them, we should be grateful and enjoy what we have worked for."

This concept is easier said than done. Funny enough, we had been ministering to another couple of the importance of rest – that when we rest in Him and His Word, *then* He is able to do what only He can do; problem is we hadn't been following this principal ourselves up to this point. We shared scripture such as:

Matthew 11:28-30 "Come to Me all who labor and are heavy laden, and I will give you rest. Take My yoke upon you, and learn from Me, for I am gentle and lowly in heart, and you will find rest for your souls. For My yoke is easy, and My burden is light."
Psalm 127:2 "it is vain that you rise up early and go late to rest, eating the bread of anxious toil; for He gives to His beloved sleep."

This one was particularly humorous for us to share given our past few years I just told you about. We knew the Word of God, but we knew nothing about rest. At least, not until He called us to this desolate place to…rest a while. And when we did, it changed our life.

Mark 6:31 "And he said to them, 'Come away by yourselves to a desolate place and rest a while.' For many were coming and going, and they had no leisure even to eat."

So, here's how it happened. There was one week in particular which I was just having an extremely hard time. We had been consistently driving out of town every Saturday to meet up with some friends in ministry. We would meet with them every Saturday to fellowship, but this week I had a breakdown; I felt like I was drowning in life and helpless. I felt like the past five years I had been running around in a hamster wheel, going nowhere, and *waiting* for life to start, because surely, this was not it. I text my friend and asked her to pray for me and told her that I was likely going to stay home that coming Saturday. What I didn't know is they had already planned a surprise for us for that very weekend. They didn't give us any heads-up about it because they knew we *always* showed up, every Saturday, without fail. She urged me to come anyway but I really had already made it up in my mind to stay home.

Well, they convinced me to come and to pack a bag to stay. I was a bit perplexed but at this point I was so emotionally drained that my mind was pretty much shut off and I felt like I was functioning on autopilot. So, I packed a bag and got in the car, and we drove. Our friends sent us an address to show up to.

We arrive at this huge three-story home on the river. Confused and still trying to gain our bearings, we begin to walk up the stairs. At the top of the second staircase stood a woman I had never seen before wearing a long flowing dress in my favorite color, coral. Her blonde hair lit up from the sun shining through the window behind her. If you recall, I am not a big hugger, but for some reason, in this state of autopilot I'm in, I approach this woman and hug her immediately. I shocked myself. I didn't *know* her! I don't even hug people I know! I don't know who she is or why she's there! I don't even know why *I'm* there!

Turns out she is a friend of our friends' who they themselves had just met in person a couple of days prior. She had just sold her home and wanted to bless them with a vacation home to stay together and fellowship, and she told them to invite *us*! Why us? She didn't know us. She didn't really know *any* of us! Little did I know this is a woman who I had, in fact, spoken to one time on a phone call with these friends of ours. The Lord gave me a prophetic word for her on that call, that where she was about to move to is where she would find the relationships she's been looking for and longing for. I felt in my spirit that I was going to be one of those friends, but I never said that part out loud because it didn't make sense to me. She didn't live near me, wasn't planning on moving near me, not to mention, *I didn't know this woman!!*

Realizing that, it began to make sense why I was drawn to her immediately. From that moment our friendship grew. We talked about hair, experiences in the church, giving so much just to be rejected by those we helped, dealing with stress, the importance of self-care. We would wake up and have coffee on the rooftop overlooking the river, sit at the end of the dock watching the dolphins swim by, laugh, and talk about the Lord. We spent hours in the evenings in the rooftop hot tub, talking and bonding over our many similarities and how we're both nuts but how God loves nuts. I was so inspired, not only by her generosity and selflessness to share this beautiful experience with complete strangers, but her obedience to, and love for, the Lord.

Her wealth of knowledge of the Word of God was so impressive and the way she, as spiritually deep as she is, accepted me with my tattoos, though I tried by best to shamefully hide them, was so refreshing and affirming for me. My friendship with this woman has healed so many broken places in me in the most organic way. She never once judged me for my tattoos as many seasoned Christians would – and do. She told me she saw a lot of herself in me, in the hunger we both have for seeking the *truth* and the *genuine* will of God. She said she would be the shoulders for me to stand on to surpass even that which she has achieved in relationship with the Lord. This is so unheard of to me, and I would say, to most people. Not many people will *want* to push someone else to elevate higher than them. Let me tell you, this woman is one-of-one. There is nobody like her!

Some other friends flew in to stay with us for one night as they had to be back home for work on Monday. We were talking to them about how hard they were working themselves between their job and their home business. We ministered to them about the importance of rest. Funny, coming from us, when my husband works just as hard and just as often. They took it in but insisted on making it home to get back to work.

As the days progressed, we were having such good fellowship and such a good time together that we decided to extend our stay at the house. Meanwhile my husband continued going to work, as the rest of the house was trying to convince him to just take some time off and enjoy the time we were able to be there. We both were reluctant to the idea but realized we can't preach about rest to others and be unwilling to do it ourselves.

We both realized that we had to just jump by faith. At that moment we both agreed that he should take that rest of the day off. By that point we had already been blessed more than I could have ever expected by a woman who didn't even know us, had never met us, but rented this beautiful, vacation home and invited us to come stay, I was in total awe; but I *never* could have expected the blessing that I believe was released as a direct result of that decision we had made to rest and put our trust in the Lord.

As a direct result of us resting in the Lord, we received funding for our businesses and to launch our ministry just a month later, which allowed my husband to quit his job and for us to move back to the beach to a condo. We couldn't afford it. We didn't ask for it. We *never* could have made it happen! But God had it all lined up from the very beginning. He turned it all around in an instant!

My husband was committed to accepting and staying at the miserable job the Lord had for him, even when it didn't make sense. That job connected us to not only the woman who sent my husband to get his doctorate, but also the friends we stayed at the vacation home with who introduced us to my new bestie (who did end up moving near us, by the way) and ultimately, it all led to the blessing that took us out of our season of struggle.

All we had to do was to have *faith*, trust God, *obey* in the simple things and *rest*. Because when we finally take our hands off His plan and let Him have control, He can do far more in a moment of our rest, than we could ever do over years and years of hard work and toil. Our turnaround was immediate. *Immediate!* He knew from the very beginning where our breakthrough was, He was always going to get us to it, and it was always in His perfect time. Give it to Him, He wants to take the burden from you.

I could have never imagined a blessing like this! And if you recall, I *almost* didn't even show up for that weekend! That is just like the enemy, when your biggest breakthrough blessing is *right* around the corner, he will try to discourage you and get into your head and try to make you give up. But I thank God for His Word, both in scripture and through the prophets, that encouraged me to make it through and not give up. To be patient and know that God has got it all in control. I had been on the verge of giving up so many times; on my marriage, on life. I wanted to run away and start over, at the same time I wanted to end it all. But glory be to God for giving me the courage to push through into His place of rest.

Exodus 33:14 "And He said, 'My presence will go with you, and I will give you rest.'"

He wants to give you rest. But you have to believe that and be willing to receive it. There is no need to stress. If the storm is going to come, it's coming whether you stress or not. The good news is, He's with you. Regardless of what you are going through, keep Him close and *He* will give you rest, *He* will make you dwell in safety. You *can* endure. You can sleep soundly. You dwell in His safety.

Psalm 4:8 "In peace I will both lie down and sleep; for You alone, O Lord, make me dwell in safety."

I have come to realize through this journey that after years of sacrificing comfort for saving and doing the absolute minimum to enjoy life in an attempt to get ahead only to get nowhere, from now on we will try to just trust in His promise and enjoy the ride. It's not easy, I don't believe it ever will be easy to have full faith in our ability to rest, but life is too short not to enjoy one another and the time we have together.

Zechariah 8:7-8 "I will rescue my people from the lands where they have been taken and will bring them back — They will be my people, and I will be their God, ruling over them faithfully and justly."

We went through the wringer! But we needed it, I know I needed it for *sure*. I will always be thankful for every lesson I learned in the wilderness and always carry this appreciation I have for the person the Lord has made me. And now, just as He said He would, He has rescued us.

My Testimony

I truly, genuinely believed I was the least likely to receive a promise like this, but I am proof to myself and hopefully proof to someone else going through it right now, that if we *actually* do what He asks, and follow His guidelines, He *will* do what He has promised! It doesn't matter how ridiculous and impossible it might seem to you. You don't have to understand it for it to be true. It takes faith and it takes patience, but it is so worth it!

So don't despise the pain of the process and reject Him, pay close attention to your season in the valley; it was meant for you to *learn* from. It was intended to strengthen your faith! The journey of pain we as family went through, was a challenging process building patience, faith, and humility. All so He could position us in His Kingdom, not by our might or strength, but complete obedience and faith in God.

So, believe me when I tell you, our struggles may be different, they may be very similar, but I have been through the fire, and these are the things that have helped bring me out. I hope and pray they help you, too. The humility of enduring the devastating process was hard, however we could have aborted our blessings if we attempted to be self-righteous and elevate ourselves, yet we trusted God and remained in faith.

Will you trust God in the devastating areas of your life? If you do, your humility and faith is transportation to your blessing, if you trust Him. He has begun to bring these promises to pass in my life and I believe that He will continue do exactly what He said He would do, and He will do it for you, too!

I began writing these things down for myself, to remember this brand-new journey vividly; to never forget what God had done along the way or how I felt at the time, then it came to a point where I realized it could be helpful insight for someone else, so I turned my story into a book. I think that too often "Christians" do too much telling, shaming, and condemning and not enough encouraging, uplifting, and guiding by example. I see so many people on social media with the perception that every "Karen" or racist is a Christian, and I hate that the church has been given that stereotype, but I would be lying if I said that wasn't my initial thought as well; but y'all don't let rude nasty people keep you off social media, so why let them keep you from the love of God?

I refuse to tell someone to do something I haven't done myself or speak on something I have never been through personally, which is why I tell this story from my own personal account; not to tell anyone what they "should do" but rather, what I "have done", how it worked out, and how you can do it too.

Here   are   some   tips...

Part 1

How to Deal: *With Your Past*

Chapter 2

Don't Dwell on the Pain of the Past

Isaiah 43:18 "Do not cling to events of the past or dwell on what happened long ago."

Don't let your past hold you back from what God has already promised for your future. Whatever pain you're carrying with you from the past, whether it was ten minutes ago or ten years ago, let it go! It's okay to mourn and grieve but don't get stuck there, you've got to know when to start looking ahead. Choose today to feel all the feels. Go ahead and blast your sad songs and cry one last time, eat a tub of ice cream sprinkled with tears and wallow in self-pity.

How to Deal: *With Your Past*

James 4:9-10 "Be sorrowful, cry, and weep; change your laughter into crying, your joy into gloom! Humble yourselves before the Lord, and He will lift you up."

This scripture contextually has a different meaning, but it still applies. Quit trying to fake it! Go ahead and let it out; however you like to cope, go ahead and do it – but once this day is over you have to move on. You've got to make the conscious decision to quit holding on; drop it and let it *go*. That is the point where God is able to lift you up. That time is now!

Philippians 3:13 "Of course, my friends, I really do not think that I have already won it; the one thing I do, however, is to forget what is behind me and do my best to reach what is ahead."

The pain was tough, no doubt; but there is something better ahead. The only way to reach it is to leave it behind and push forward. People are going to hurt you, whether intentionally or unintentionally, but either way, it's all part of the process. God will use it for your good!

People are strategically placed in your life to do a work in you; you cannot stop it and you cannot change it. All you can do is look for the growth in it. Growing up, my dad never kept his word and didn't protect me when I needed him, but through that, I've learned to manage expectations, always stand up for myself, and always, *always* keep my word. Ex boyfriends cheated on me and treated me *horribly* and for the life of me I could not understand why. After I left them, they chased after me for *years* and when I confronted them about why they treated me so wrong in the first place they could not even try to piece together why; but all the pain from those relationships gave me the foundation to truly see and appreciate the man I had in front of me when I was dating my now husband.

People I befriended in church betrayed me and said nasty, horrible, untrue things about me, and although I wanted to get offended and leave the "church of hypocrites", as I perceived it, it taught me to understand that these people are not God, Christians are not God, even pastors are not God, and they do not represent the church or God and they do *not* have the authority to make me question my faith or walk away from my church.

I could go on and on with examples of pain caused by people which had a purpose in my life. The point is, nothing that has happened to you is a surprise to God; it's all part of His Master Plan. Let Him use it! As painful as some things in my life were, I will never allow them to tarnish my future in a negative way; in every one of those examples, I *chose* to receive the good from them. I don't look at God through the experiences of my dad and I don't look at the church through the experiences I had with other Christians. I don't look at my husband through the experiences of my exes but have so much appreciation for him *because* of those experiences.

I fully understand now that they treated me so horribly because they were never meant for me, and I never would have left otherwise. I mean, if God had told me before I met any one of them, "Ok, I'm going to send you this guy, you're going to like him a lot, he's going to make your heart beat fast and your stomach flutter and all that, but he's going to treat you very badly. He's going to go out without you most nights and not come home at all occasionally, cheat on you with many women, disrespect you, etc., but he's *exactly* who you deserve." I'd be like, um, God, are You ok? Ahhm…rude!! But that's not the case. See, these were *never* the men God had for me, and He knew what it would take to make me leave.

The problem is, I'm a tough and loyal chick, which is a terrible combination in these toxic situations, because I would stay loyal through abuse – I can take it, and I can give it. If you disrespect me verbally, I can dish it back 100-fold. My thick skin can tolerate disrespectful words. But as my mother's only daughter, I was the princess of the household –

Don't Dwell on the Pain of the Past

I never learned to share, so cheating is just something I will not tolerate. So, you see, it's all about perspective. It was all working for my good all along, so I take the good and leave the bad back there with them, in my past.

Sometimes we veer off from His plan, it's easy to let these hurtful events derail us, but He can always turn it back around for our good. So, don't dwell on the why or the how; why did you treat me this way? How could you do this to me? Why did this happen to me, God? Don't waste your time seeking closure, instead seek God; what can I do better, God? What can I do to glorify Your Name in this situation? What can I do to strengthen my faith? What steps do I take today, Holy Spirit? What is Your will for my life, Lord? Where do I go from here? Remember, when God gives you a new beginning, it starts with an ending. Be thankful for closed doors, they often lead to the right one. Trust Him.

Isaiah 30:19-21 "The Lord is compassionate, and when you cry to Him for help, He will answer you. The Lord will make you go through hard times, but He Himself will be there to teach you, and you will not have to search for Him anymore. If you wander off the road to the right or the left, you will hear His voice behind you saying, 'Here is the road. Follow it.'"

How to Deal: *With Your Past*

Ecclesiastes 6:10 "Everything that happens was already determined long ago, and we all know that you cannot argue with someone who is stronger than you."

"*Everything* that happens..." Not *some* things, not every *good* thing – *every*thing! Have you ever had someone come into your life that hurt you so badly, someone you trusted, someone who was supposed to love you and protect you, and they just tore your whole world apart and they themselves couldn't even explain why? You guys, some people are placed in our lives to teach us, to correct us, to prepare us and sometimes to give us our testimony to share with others and help them to overcome in the future. As bad as it may seem at times, *nothing* is done without God's approval.

Revelation 3:7 "He has the key that belonged to David, and when He opens a door, no one can close it, and when He closes it, no one can open it."

There is always a greater glory at the end if you'll just trust in Him and hold strong in your faith. You would understand it if you could see the big picture how God sees it. I look back on the most painful events in my life and I can literally connect the dots on how they have all worked together to get me to where I am today. Without all that pain,

Don't Dwell on the Pain of the Past

I never could have appreciated or even known the incredible indescribable peace, which the Lord brings to those who love Him. Sometimes God has to do something *in* us before He does something *for* us.

It makes absolutely no sense in the natural, the kind of peace that I feel now in this painful season, and I'm still in it! But that's the power of God. As I write this today, I'm still living in a one-bedroom apartment with my boyfriend and daughter and barely getting by, but I'm at peace. I'm still buying my groceries from the Dollar Tree, but I'm at peace. I'm still washing our clothes by hand in the kitchen sink and wringing them out until my hands blister and bleed, but I'm at peace. I'm keeping my head up and looking ahead because I know that God's got me. So, look *forward* to it, literally! Keep your eyes on the road ahead.

Luke 9:62 "Anyone who starts to plow and then keeps looking back is of no use for the Kingdom of God."

You've got to let it *go!* You cannot move forward if you keep on looking back. You will trip and you *will* fall. People will sit around crying out and praying to God to come change their situation and heal their pain, but they don't want to do their part. It reminds me of an ex that I had a particularly hard time getting over. Although I had left him and it was very clearly a toxic relationship that I so badly wanted to get over, I would keep looking at old photos and listening to songs that reminded me of him and think of the times we spent together. I was trying so hard to let go but I wouldn't actually let it go!

God won't take away your pain if you won't let it go. Quit replaying those same old songs. Let go of your pain, let go of your shattered expectations, let go of what was, and look forward to what is to come. Look ahead to what God has in store for you in the future. What God wants to do for you is *always* better than anything you could do for yourself. So don't dwell on relationships that didn't work out, people who let you down or abused you, unexpected events, illnesses, or loss.

Ecclesiastes 3:14 "I know that everything God does will last forever. You can't add anything or take anything away from it."

...so quit trying! If it has already happened, there is nothing you can do now to take it back; it has already been done, and it was done according to God's pre-determined plan. Don't dwell on what you could have done differently, you didn't! It's okay! You can't change the past, but God can change your perspective. Anything that God takes away or breaks down, He will always return to us much greater than before, *if* you're obedient through the process.

Take Job for example, Job was a man who did seemingly everything right and had it all! Seven sons, three daughters, seven thousand sheep, three thousand camels, one thousand head of cattle, five hundred donkeys, large number of servants and on top of all that he was the richest man in the East. Then, Satan stepped in. He asked God to *allow* him to test Job's faithfulness to Him, saying that He has always given Job so much, if He was to take away everything he has, Job would curse God to His face, and the Lord agreed on one condition, Satan was not allowed to physically hurt Job.

Job 1:12 "'All right,' the Lord said to Satan, 'everything he has is in your power, but you must not hurt Job yourself.' So Satan left."

Job only experienced these attacks because God *allowed* them, and Satan was only interested in Job *because* he was so good. So, when people ask the question, "If God is so good, why do bad things happen to good people?" The enemy doesn't attack you if you have no value; as they say, thieves don't break into empty houses. So, God allowing for Satan's attacks does not mean God is a cruel sadist.

God Himself did not *cause* the attacks, but He allowed them because He was so sure of Job's strength, faithfulness, and willingness to endure and He had an even greater blessing in mind for Job in the end, as long as he was obedient and willing to endure the process. Could it be that God has the same sureness in us and our strength and faith to allow us to be tested? And let me tell you, Satan let Job have it: his donkeys and camels were stolen; his sheep, shepherds and servants were all killed; his own children were all killed in a storm! And his response to all of this devastating news was:

Job 1:21 "I was born with nothing, and I will die with nothing. The Lord gave, and now He has taken away. May His Name be praised!"

This is probably the most important and yet the most difficult concept to fully understand. The Lord is the reason we have anything at all, including our life, so when the time comes for it to end, whether for us or our loved ones, it was a blessing for us to have even had it at all. The Lord gives, and the Lord takes away. You were born with nothing, and you will die with nothing. You have no control on when you enter this world or when you leave it. Now that mentality still takes some serious faith and strength for *sure,* but it is possible to get there.

Don't Dwell on the Pain of the Past

The book of Job was the first I had ever read in the Bible, and I could really relate to a lot of what he was going through. Job endured a lot of sudden loss, chaos, and destruction in a short amount of time. Job's faith in God continued on for a while as Satan tempted him, meanwhile his wife is telling him to just curse God and die, but Job refused. Over some time, however, Job's thoughts began to turn dark, he began to question God, and get real with Him.

Job 6:8 "Why won't God give me what I ask? Why won't He answer my prayer?"

Don't we all feel this way sometimes? I mean, you can endure so much for so long but at some point, you just reach a level of frustration and hopelessness and just say, Lord, what's up?? You mad?? In the end, after all he had endured, when Job humbled himself, set himself and all his troubles aside and prayed for his three friends, the Bible says it was then, that the Lord made him prosperous again and gave him twice as much as he had before and that He blessed the last part of Job's life even more than He had blessed the first.

This is the goodness of God when we remain faithful to Him under trials; the devil loves to take what's great and ruin it, but God loves to take what is ruined and make it great! And as obedient and faithful as Job was to the Lord in the beginning, it wasn't until after these trials that Job *really* knew God for himself.

Job 42:5 "In the past I knew only what others had told me, but now I have seen You with my own eyes."

Sometimes God will use these trials in order to bring us closer to Him. I know for me, it took losing everything and almost my life, then seeing it restored, for me to truly see God with my own eyes. If life had kept going decently bad and sometimes good for me, I wouldn't have sought God. Never. I would have continued to live my empty, selfish life, never knowing that there was more. God has a purpose for everything and can give purpose to *anything!* Whatever the reason may be, let's all move forward together, endure our season, and receive Job's double blessing for *our* lives!

Alright! So, now that the crying is over and the pain is in the past, (right?) it's time to get your groove back! Ladies, if you wear makeup, make your face up! Even just to walk around the house if you've got nowhere to go (or you can't find a sitter – *sigh*...) it can still make a woman feel better just to see herself put together again; sometimes if ya look good, ya feel good! Try a dramatic new hairstyle change, chop it off or get some extensions, try a new color, get together with your girls (but *don't* talk about the issue), buy yourself some daring new shoes, a bold new dress, splurge on some designer jeans that make you feel *fierce* or even a designer bag if you've got the cash.

Luke 12:33 "Provide for yourselves purses that don't wear out."

That scripture really speaks to me – it says, *Louis Vuitton*. Kidding! Kind of. But really, just treat yourself! Even if you don't have much to spend, make it a point to set some cash aside to spoil yourself. Whatever makes *you* feel good, do it! If you used to enjoy painting, paint! If you like dancing, get out there and dance! If exercising is your thing, get back to it! Men, buy yourself some new gear, get with some friends and get out there again, hit the gym and work on that revenge body, take your woman out, buy yourself that Corvette you've been dreaming of, if you're ballin' like that...take your old truck for a run through the mud. Do what *you* love.

Don't depend on others to get you out of your funk; nobody can take care of you like you can take care of you! Make yourself a priority! Go ahead and let loose (within reason) it's okay to go out for a drink with some friends, you know, for your digestion.

1 Timothy 5:23 "Do not drink water only, but take a little wine to help your digestion, since you are sick so often."

Ecclesiastes 9:7-8 "Go ahead — eat your food and be happy; drink your wine and be cheerful. It's all right with God. Always look happy and cheerful. Enjoy life with the one you love."

Oh, girl! You don't have to tell me twice! Again, within reason, notice I said *a* drink, and the scripture says *a little* wine, nobody is saying getting drunk solves your problems, but it's good to let loose sometimes, however you see fit. Moderation is key!

Ephesians 5:18 "Do not get drunk with wine, which will only ruin you; instead, be filled with the Spirit."

Yes, Sir! Now of course, you don't have to *forget* your past. It's *okay* to look back every once and a while, but don't get stuck there! Get it all out one good time and then look back on it only as a lesson. It is your testimony, you are *supposed* to learn from it. See what could be learned from it, and let those lessons be the *only* things you bring with to your future. Use your story as a testimony to help others but leave the pain in the past.

Romans 5:3 "We also boast of our troubles, because we know that trouble produces endurance, endurance brings God's approval, and His approval creates hope. This hope does not disappoint us, for God has

Don't Dwell on the Pain of the Past

poured out His love into our hearts by means of the Holy Spirit, who is God's gift to us."

Don't worry about what your situation *looks* like; don't worry about what you've been through. Worry steals joy away from your future unnecessarily. Fear prolongs the process. You're going to need faith to get you through, and faith and fear cannot coexist. Don't worry about what you can't control, give it up to God, put Him in control. It's in God's hands anyway. You are just getting in the way when you try to put your hands on it and control the outcome yourself. He sees the big picture; He has the best plan for you! It may not seem like it now, but that's where faith comes in.

Matthew 6:27 "Can any of you live a bit longer by worrying about it?"

Of course, you can't! Worry does you no good. The enemy wants you to worry about what's next so you can't enjoy what's now. The devil is a liar, don't let that punk win! Why stress yourself out being worried about something you cannot predict? Worry and stress will steal your life! How many times have you worried about something that never even happened?

Guys, I literally look back at all the things I stressed about and lost sleep over along this journey and looking back now, I wish I would have just relaxed and enjoyed the ride the best I could. Everything that happened was going to happen regardless of how I felt or what negative thoughts I replayed in my head. All the worrying I did never changed one thing. It didn't need to be half as miserable as it was if I'd just quit worrying about every little thing.

Job 5:2 "To worry yourself to death with resentment would be a foolish, senseless thing to do."
Matthew 6:34 "So do not worry about tomorrow; it will have enough worries of its own. There is no need to add to the troubles each day brings."

Focus on today! God does not want you to worry! He makes that very clear! Be so confident in His plan that you don't even get upset anymore when things don't go your way. This is the true test of your walk with God – when you don't understand anything at all and trust Him anyway.

You've just got to trust in His plan, He doesn't need you to figure it all out. I think about my daughter – every time we go somewhere, she wants to know where we're going, what we're doing, how long we're going to be there, what we're doing after that...I'm like, ma'am...you're

92

twelve…do you have some place to be? Preexisting plans, we are unaware of? No? Okay then, just *ride*. You don't need to worry about all the details. She concerns herself with *everything*. This child will check behind me about everything *I* do… "Did you lock the door?" "What's for dinner?" "Did you buy bread at the store?" and my favorite, the *very moment* the gas light comes on in the car, from the back seat, "You need gas." *OKAY!* I'm like, wow, please tell me at what point in my thirty-one years of life and fourteen years of being on my own do *I* get to be an adult?

Lord…it's funny, but I feel like God feels the same way about us. At what point are we going to quit checking behind God and let Him be God. "Well, God, did you remember to line up a job for me? You know I need to pay my bills." "Did you remember to defend me from those people who did me wrong? I left it to You like You asked me to." God has been God a lot longer than you've been around; let Him be God. Just *ride*.

The Lord has put you through this season either to test you, correct you, or bless you, but either way, He wants to bring you out better. Although it may seem like a punishment sent straight from the depths of hell, you've got to trust in God, surrender to Him, increase your faith, focus on your praise, and pass this test!

Job 33:19 "God corrects us by sending sickness and filling our bodies with pain."

Please hear me loud and clear, sickness is by no means *always* sent by God or *always* a means for correction or *always* because of something *you* did or need to do. Consider the man in John chapter 9 who was born blind; Jesus' disciples asked Jesus, "Who sinned that he would be born blind, him or his parents?" Sin and generational curses are certainly a possibility, however Jesus answered them, "neither this man nor his parents sinned, but this happened so that the works of God might be displayed in him." God will allow certain things in order to correct you, and you've got to be willing to learn and accept what He is trying to achieve in you. Perhaps He will use it to display His works, but will you trust Him? Will you call on Him or just lay down? He may send us sickness, and if you just get upset and curse God and boo-hoo your way through it, then all you've got is sickness; but if you are obedient and ask God what He wants you to do and evaluate what you need to change, He can heal you and bring you out of it even better than you were before.

Well, why would God send us sickness? Have you ever noticed how it often takes a disaster to bring divided communities together? Or how some families will have arguments or disagreements or hateful feelings toward each other for years, and often times it takes sickness and sometimes even a death in the family to bring those people together and understand how much they really mean to each other? There are many reasons God may use sickness within us, but it's up to you to reflect on your own life as to why and what may need to change. Maybe it's a sign to stop worrying. Worry and stress have been known to cause many health issues; learn to put your faith in Him.

Job 5:17-18 "Happy is the person whom God corrects! Do not resent it when He rebukes you. God bandages the wounds He makes; His hand hurts you, and His hand heals."

Keep your peace and your faith high through the storm. Do not resist this teaching, no matter how hard it may seem; you will end up blocking your blessings if you quit now. Stick with Him, He will bandage the wounds He makes, if you let Him. Don't get angry with God for bringing this season upon you. Now, you should be *honest* with Him, because He does ask that you worship Him in spirit and truth.

John 4:24 "God is a Spirit: and they that worship Him must worship Him in spirit and in truth." KJV

I received a prophetic word this past week like I had never received before. Part of what God was telling me, through this woman at a conference, was that I've been asking Him, "When, God? When, God? When will my season change? When are my blessings coming? When, God?" And He was saying, "I love that about you, you are honest with Me, and I love that about you. Your season is here, I am going to answer your prayers." (Looking back now, He sure did!) but God wants you to be *real* with Him. Tell Him what you really want, tell Him how you really feel. Be *real*. Forget about the "Dear God, it's me, Desirée. Thou art Your servant at thine feet to worship thee…" First of all, He knows it's you, okay. Second, He is our friend, He is with us and for us. Talk to Him like He is your friend sitting right in front of you. "God, this feels *impossible!* I am lost, I *need* You!! Help me!!" It doesn't have to be epic.

So, accept this discipline, take a look at yourself, at your life; is there something you need to change? Are you being kind to everyone, are you forgiving, are you walking by faith and not by sight, are you loving everyone, meaning *everyone*, as you love yourself? Not all trauma is brought on by our own doing, but some surely are. Evaluate yourself, honestly. Make the necessary changes and ask for God's help along the way. When the road gets tough, tell Him, and ask Him where to go, what to do, He wants to guide you.

Don't Dwell on the Pain of the Past

Zephaniah 3:2 "[You have] not listened to the Lord or accepted His discipline. [You have] not put [your] trust in the Lord or asked for His help."

You put all your burdens and your trust in people who are sick and tired of hearing about it, and you post it all over your social media, yet you won't take it to God, the one who actually *wants* to hear it and can truly help you through anything. Remember, nothing happens without God's approval, good or bad! God will take you through the "wilderness" to get you to your blessings, your family doesn't know the reason, your friends and followers don't know the reason, your therapist doesn't even know the reason, but God does; all He asks for is your *faith* through the process.

Matthew 4:1 "Then the Spirit led Jesus into the wilderness to be tempted by the devil."

Don't take it personal; He brought Jesus through it, what makes you think you won't have to endure it as well? There are going to be temptations along the way, but don't get distracted, remember, God does not tempt you, any temptation is from the devil, so you've got to hold strong and resist the devil and he will flee.

James 1:13 "For God cannot be tempted by evil, and He Himself tempts no one."
James 4:7 "Submit yourselves therefore to God. Resist the devil, and he will flee from you." KJV

The word "flee" is defined as, "To go swiftly or escape, as from danger. To pass away swiftly. To run away or try to escape from." I believe that if you resist the devil long enough and consistently, he will not only run in fear from you, but all his plans and plots against you will pass away swiftly and they will be done away with; it can happen in an instant! When the devil sees your strength in Christ, he gets scared, you become dangerous! You no longer have to try to outrun him; he will be trying to escape from you.

So, submit yourself to God and turn from sin as often as you possibly can. Do your best to live right with God, it's a lifestyle. Always be praising His Name, even through your biggest struggles; your car breaks down, "Thank You, Jesus for what You kept me from." Your kids are acting up, "Thank You, Jesus, my kids are alive, and their lungs are healthy." You lose your job, "Thank You, Jesus for the new employment opportunity You have for me." Don't let the devil drive that wedge between you and your Savior, your Answer, your Direction, your Hope; you need Him!

98

Don't Dwell on the Pain of the Past

Habakkuk 3:17-19 "Even though the fig trees have no fruit and no grapes grow on the vines, even though the olive crop fails and the fields produce no grain, even though the sheep all die and the cattle stalls are empty, I will still be joyful and glad, because the Lord God is my Savior. The Sovereign Lord gives me strength. He makes me sure-footed as a deer and keeps me safe on the mountains."

Chapter 3

Don't Dwell on Choices of the Past

I had a really hard time adjusting to the "Christian" life. I never felt like I was good enough, never felt like I could measure up. I always felt like an outcast. I'm thinking, *I don't dress like these women! We can't relate. They haven't done the things I've done; Lord, imagine if they ever found out. I better wear long sleeves, so they don't see my tattoos, then they'll really know I don't belong.*

God never asked us for perfection, all He asks is to love Him, love others, and do your best. Don't be so hard on yourself! We all sin, but don't get hung up on who you were before you came to Christ. You don't have to clean yourself up before you come, He will come to you, right there in the worst of your sin. It's never too late to get right with God! Guess what, I don't have a squeaky-clean past. And if we're being honest, neither do you; we'll *never* be perfect. But God chose us, knowing the mistakes we've made and knowing He can give purpose to them and use them for our good. In knowing that, I have learned to be thankful for my past.

Ephesians 2:3-5 "Actually, all of us were like them and lived according to our natural desires, doing whatever suited the wishes of our own bodies and minds. In our natural condition we, like everyone else, were destined to suffer God's anger. But God's mercy is so abundant, and His love for us is so great, that while we were spiritually dead in our disobedience He brought us to life with Christ."

"*While* we were spiritually dead in our *disobedience*, He brought us to life..." It doesn't matter what you've done. No matter how terrible, His mercy is so abundant and love so great that He still desires to redeem us and bring us in. We all sin, sin is in our nature (thanks Adam...), but if you only believe in Him, you will be saved! He knew we were sinful, and He knows we will *still* make mistakes now and then.

Romans 3:23 "everyone has sinned and is far away from God's saving presence."
Ecclesiastes 7:20 "There is no one on earth who does what is right all the time and never makes a mistake."

This is why it upsets me so much to hear "Christians" shame other believers for "not living right" or say things like, "the scripture says...blah blah blah...you're sinning!!" Well, duh! We all are, Enid! You're the worst of them! The whole *world* is under the power of sin, that is all the more reason we must thank the Lord Jesus Christ, He's got us covered by His grace!

Galatians 3:22 "But the scripture says that the whole world is under the power of sin; and so the gift which is promised on the basis of faith in Jesus Christ is given to those who believe."

All you have to do is believe. Not perform, not put on a show, not behave a certain way – believe. Although sin is expected and His grace covers it, you still must do your best to live in right standing with God and repent for when you don't. He knows your heart and knows when you are truly trying to obey His teaching with your heart, and He knows when you're taking advantage of His mercy and grace.

Romans 6:14 "Sin must not be your master; for you do not live under Law but under God's grace."
Romans 6:17-18 "But thanks be to God! For though at one time you were slaves to sin, you have obeyed with all your heart the truth found in the teaching you received. You were set free from sin and became the slaves of righteousness."

God knows we are not perfect, we haven't been perfect since Adam and Eve; but we *can* repent, and He *will* forgive us. That's what God wants. He doesn't want us to *do this* or *don't do that* because we are told to, He wants to know that it is our hearts desire to do good, love, and be righteous. He sees our sins, He already knows every little detail of the darkest dirtiest sins in our lives, but He wants us; He wants us to repent, and He wants to forgive us.

Luke 5:32 "I have not come to call respectable people to repent, but outcasts."

God called me *as* a sinner. My journey with Christ started in a club…my first "God if You're real…" prayer was answered…in a club. God does not avoid the sinners and the outcasts and the rebellious people, He calls on them. He doesn't avoid the bars, clubs, trap houses and prisons, His beloved people are there. He can call you from anywhere, and I am so thankful that He called me because I sure wasn't going to just drop in on His doorstep by my own doing; in fact, no one can come to Christ unless God calls them, so I am *thankful* for my past, it's my greatest testimony.

Luke 19:10 "The Son of Man came to seek and to save the lost."
John 6:44 "People cannot come to Me unless the Father who sent Me draws them to Me; and I will raise them to life on the last day."
John 6:37 "Everyone my Father gives Me will come to Me. I will never turn away anyone who comes to Me."

How to Deal: *With Your Past*

God knows, before we're even born, exactly what each of us needs individually. *He* seeks *us, He* calls *us.* I've lived the wild and carefree, crazy party life, and take it from me, it's not all it's cracked up to be. Now, being saved, I'm thankful for those experiences, because having already lived "that life," I know that I'm not missing out. I know that God has the best life in store for me if I will just go through the process and leave the rest behind.

Galatians 1:15-17 "But God in His grace chose me even before I was born, and called me to serve Him. And when He decided to reveal His Son to me, so that I might preach the Good News about Him to the Gentiles, I did not go to anyone for advice, nor did I go to Jerusalem to see those who were apostles before me."

You guys I have no idea what I'm doing; not really! I am a brand-new Christian, I wasn't raised up in a church, I'm not a theologian, I opened a Bible for the first time in my life five months ago from the day I write these words! I have no official spiritual training, I'm not certified in any kind of teaching, I'm not an experienced author, I don't even know how I'll get this book out to the public; but when the Lord put it in my heart to share the Good News, to share my experience, to glorify His Kingdom and to share my testimony, I didn't stop to ask anyone for advice or permission, the only help I need was placed inside of me when I gave myself to the Lord.

1 John 2:27 "But as for you, Christ has poured out His Spirit on you. As long as His Spirit remains in you, you do not need anyone to teach you. For His Spirit teaches you about everything, and what He teaches is true, not false. Obey the Spirit's teaching, then, and remain in union with Christ."

I can tell you, as I have said many, many times in the past; I *never* would have been caught in a church or reading a Bible or living a "Christian life". I thought every Christian was a hypocrite (turns out many are, but that's between them and God), I had studied all kinds of religious conspiracy theory videos and astrologic parallels to religious beliefs, and I wasn't necessarily convinced that there was a higher power, but I *surely* didn't believe that Jesus was it. To be completely honest, I didn't care one way or the other, I was only interested in living *my* life; I was a rebellious, impulsive, wild, and carefree party animal and living for *myself.* But when you are called by God, even the biggest skeptic cannot resist answering that call.

Romans 10:20-21 "'I was found by those who were not looking for Me; I appeared to those who were not asking for Me.' 'All day long I held out My hands to welcome a disobedient and rebellious people.'"

How to Deal: *With Your Past*

I wanted nothing to do with Him you guys! I didn't want to have to be held responsible for what I did or wanted to do; I didn't want to have to answer for my wild behavior. I certainly didn't want to be judged by other "Christians" for every little move I made or word I spoke. I thought the whole idea of religion was crazy! I mean, I looked at these people who believed, just in awe that anyone would actually believe such silly things. I thought all religion was a cult, honestly. Although I didn't know much about it, the thought of an invisible man in the sky who you just talk to and sing to, who created the universe and everything in it and wrote this book that everyone is supposed to follow was just not even on the spectrum of what I was about to believe. And then they're always asking for your money and then speaking in tongues? Forget about it! I mean, it *sounds* crazy!

For those of you who had faith before trials, props to you, man...but sometimes you can never really know until you actually live it. Sometimes you never see Him until you hit the very bottom of the bottom and have no choice but to look up. In those times, if you really study the stories in the Bible, and you start to see parallels with what you're going through, and you can have faith that you will come out victorious just as they did, and then you start to actually see it play out in your life, you guys...there is no denying that God

106

is behind it! And the best part is, no one is too far gone to be saved by God's grace.

Romans 11:6 "His choice is based on His grace, not on what they have done. For if God's choice were based on what people do, then His grace would not be real grace."

I am forever thankful to God for His grace. It's almost hard to believe that after the life some of us have lived, He will still call us to Him, and He will never turn us away. But that's the truth! That's not my assumption, that's God's Word! So, don't get hung up on your past; God doesn't, why should you?

Psalm 103:12 "As far as the east is from the west, so far does He remove our sins from us."
Hebrews 8:12 "For I [the Lord] will forgive their wickedness, and I will never again remember their sins." NIV

I have plenty of things from my past that I could be ashamed of, but I'm not! Every move I have ever made, good or bad, has made me who I am now, and it has given me a perspective and an appreciation that I never could have known without it. It has given me a testimony and a tool to relate to others who are still in it and connect with them from a very real place of understanding. I may not always relate to life-long Christians, but that's okay, because they're already saved. I'd much rather be able to relate to the lost and the broken, they're the ones that really need my fellowship.

People may look at me now or look at my past, at who I was and what I've done, and judge; but you have got to keep in mind that you have *no* idea where someone has been or what they had been through before they came to Christ and how God will use those experiences for His glory. And the coolest thing about it for me, is I have the perspective now, to *never* judge *anyone* based on their past, because I *know* what God can do.

Romans 9:25-26 "The people who were not Mine I will call 'My People' — And in the very place where they were told, 'You are not my people,' there they will be called the children of the living God."

The very people religious "Christians" look down on with judgement and reject saying they are not God's people; those are the real children of God. He loves them! You can be a child of God just as you are, right now! In the streets, in the crack house, in prison, in the club, He wants you! It doesn't matter what anyone else says, they may say you can't be a Christian until you stop drinking, you can't be a Christian until you're off drugs, God won't accept you until you stop sinning, you can't dress that way as a Christian, Christians shouldn't act that way – no!

In the very place you are told you are not His people, right there in your sin, God calls you, His children. God alone makes that call, not anyone else. And once you understand in your spirit that you are a child of God, nothing anybody tells you can keep you from that truth. God, in His time, will evolve you into what He needs you to be; He will make you a new being in Christ, but for now He *loves* you right where you are. Don't let who you were, or even who you are today, keep you from who God is allowing you to become.

2 Corinthians 5:17 "Anyone who is joined to Christ is a new being; the old is gone, the new has come. All this is done by God, who through Christ changed us from enemies into His friends and gave us the task of making others His friends also."

Do not allow others to keep you from making God *your* friend; He's the best friend you could have! I know how corny that sounds you guys, okay, but it is so true! I have spent my whole life confiding in my friends for all my troubles and it never did me much good. Friends will turn on you, betray you, and don't have all the answers anyway! God will never turn on you, and He has *all* the answers.

How to Deal: *With Your Past*

Since I have included Christ in my daily life and turned to Him in my struggles I honestly have so much peace! Oh my gosh, I used to be a complete psychopath, set off by the littlest things; my temper was out of control and now, at the time I would think my anger would be worse than ever, all I have is peace. The unexplainable peace that surpasses all understanding.

So don't let your past or what people say about it hold you back. If you look at me now, you'd see that my past has brought with me everything from tattoos that some "Christians" look down on and others may judge, to my style that I don't believe I should have to change or even hide just because I have come to Christ; and until I see something in God's Word that says otherwise, I won't! That's one of the biggest things that kept me from relationship with God in the first place - judgmental "Christians" but please understand, *they* are impossible to please, God is not.

People are going to judge you and put you down no matter what you do, that's just the reality. I could have my skin covered head to toe topped with a trench coat, and that's acceptable, but the minute I match that same "conservative" outfit with some cute thigh-high boots people feel it's their place to judge and say I need to "tone it down" because it might "cause some Christians to stray". Child of God, please.

Don't Dwell on Choices of the Past

I am a firm believer that grown adult humans have control of, and should be accountable for, their own thoughts and actions and Christian's are no exception. My mother has always raised me that way and, it's not scriptural. The Bible does say, however:

James 2:9 "But if you treat people according to their outward appearance, you are guilty of sin and the Law condemns you as a lawbreaker."

The Bible gives us a few guidelines in which to follow regarding the way we dress, but it is also very clear that it is not up to us to judge or treat people any differently according to their outward appearance. A lot of people perceive this to only apply regarding social class and to "treat the janitor as you would treat the CEO" so to speak, however, it does not specify that way. You cannot treat anyone any differently or judge them based on their outward appearance or the way they dress, in any form, period; whether you agree with it or not. Do not go beyond God's teaching. God was very thorough when He inspired the creation of the Bible; if you have concerns or opinions and the Bible does not speak of it, then it is not up to you to create distinctions.

How to Deal: *With Your Past*

2 John 9 "Anyone who does not stay with the teaching of Christ, but goes beyond it, does not have God."
Colossians 2:4 "I tell you, then, do not let anyone deceive you with false arguments, no matter how good they seem to be."

Know. The Word. For. Yourself! That way you cannot be misguided! Anyone that tells you that you must do a certain thing in order to live in right standing with God and can't lead you to the scripture to back it up in God's Word itself, is going beyond the teaching of Christ, no matter who they are or how good their argument may sound.

Romans 10:1-2 "My friends, how I wish with all my heart that my own people might be saved! How I pray to God for them! I can assure you that they are deeply devoted to God; but their devotion is not based on true knowledge."

It really feels that way in the church sometimes. Fellow believers and church goers – those are my people, and concerning some of them, I wish with all my heart that my own people might be saved! Sure, they attend church every week, they might serve, they might pray and spend time with the Lord and read scripture every day, deeply devoted to God, but if their devotion is not based on true knowledge but false teaching or routine, then their actions can be harsh, abrasive, meanspirited, and quite simply, wrong! That is why it is important to know that regardless of what people say, good or bad, it is not our goal to please them, but God.

1 Thessalonians 2:4 "We do not try to please people, but to please God, who tests our motives."
Romans 16:17-18 "I urge you, my friends: watch out for those who cause divisions and upset people's faith and go against the teaching which you have received. Keep away from them!"

There will always be people who are going to judge you, people are going to try to upset your faith and call it "God's work" but keep away from them; do not let them get to you! Stand firm in the teaching, the scripture-based Word-of-God teaching, that you receive from the Bible itself. And if someone teaches you otherwise or convicts you of something the Word of God never does, then be sure of your source. It should always be the Word of God, not man.

Matthew 11:18-19 "When John came, he fasted and drank no wine, and everyone said, 'He has a demon in him!' When the Son of Man came, He ate and drank, and everyone said, 'Look at this man! He is a glutton and a wine drinker, a friend of tax collectors and other outcasts!'"

The point is, people are going to judge you no matter what you do, it's been that way since the beginning of time. And honestly, the joke is on them! Because the Bible says:

Luke 15:7 "there will be more joy in Heaven over one sinner who repents than over ninety-nine respectable people who do not need to repent."

I know that I, myself, have made Heaven rejoice, so there is nothing man can tell me to put me down about how I live or what I've done. If they want to claim that they're so perfect, well, I claim my past and my sins because my repentance has created more joy in Heaven than ninety-nine of them! If you know what God says about you, nothing they say or do should be able to get you discouraged. Just be yourself and keep striving to be the best 'you' you can be.

This is what a lot of people miss, you do not have to become a cookie cutter Christian and change your personality and your whole sense of self in order to get right with God. Who do you think gave you your personality anyway? Finding Jesus doesn't mean losing yourself. There is nothing that says you must act like a "Christian", whatever that means. God isn't looking for actors, He wants *you,* authentically you!

Don't Dwell on Choices of the Past

1 Corinthians 7:23-24 "God bought you for a price [His Son]; so do not become slaves of people. My friends, each of you should remain in fellowship with God in the same condition that you were when you were called."

He wants you in the same condition you were in when you were called. There is a reason He made you uniquely you, don't lose yourself in religion. It will wear you out trying to be someone else; you'll be exhausted! I'm exhausted! Christians and religious people didn't die for you, you owe them nothing more than love. God knows how to use exactly who you are to relate to someone else who needs to see themselves in someone else, but they won't see that if you are disguising yourself as your neighbor.

For so long I wanted so badly to get rid of my tattoos, to be honest, I still do; but it should be because I want to, not because I am ashamed or feel unworthy of Christianity because I have ink in my skin. Relationship with God should not take away your joy or your identity! Now, that doesn't mean you should continue to act a fool if you were doing that before you came to Christ. There should certainly be some growth.

Romans 1:29-31 "They are filled with all kinds of wickedness, evil, greed, and vice; they are full of jealousy, murder, fighting, deceit, and

malice. They gossip and speak evil of one another; they are hateful to God, insolent, proud, and boastful; they think of more ways to do evil; they disobey their parents; they have no conscience; they do not keep their promises, and they show no kindness or pity for others."
Colossians 3:8-10&12-14 "But now you must get rid of all these things: anger, passion, and hateful feelings. No insults or obscene talk must ever come from your lips. Do not lie to one another, for you have put off the old self with its habits and have put on the new self. — So then, you must clothe yourselves with compassion, kindness, humility, gentleness, and patience. Be tolerant with one another and forgive one another whenever any of you has a complaint against someone else. — And to all these qualities add love, which binds all things together in perfect unity."

So yes, you must get rid of anger, pride, wickedness, evil, greed, fighting, deceit, murder, malice, vice, passion, gossip and hate, insults, jealousy, obscene talk and lies, and replace that with love, compassion, kindness, humility, gentleness, patience and tolerance and forgiveness for one another. It may seem like a lot, but all that God really asks of you time and time again is to love one another; that's it! If you can love God, love one another, and love yourself, then all these other things will follow in line so He can use you for special purposes.

Don't Dwell on Choices of the Past

2 Timothy 2:21-22 "Those who make themselves clean from all those evil things, will be used for special purposes, because they are dedicated and useful to their Master, ready to be used for every good deed. Avoid the passions of youth, and strive for righteousness, faith, love, and peace, together with those who with a pure heart call out to the Lord for help."

Matthew 22:37- "Jesus answered, 'Love the Lord your God with all your heart, with all your soul, and with all your mind.' This is the greatest and most important commandment. The second most important commandment is like it: 'Love your neighbor as you love yourself.' The whole Law of Moses and the teachings of the prophets depend on these two commandments."

Romans 13:8-10 "Be under obligation to no one — the only obligation you have is to love one another. Whoever does this has obeyed the Law. — 'Love your neighbor as you love yourself.' If you love others, you will never do them wrong; to love, then, is to obey the whole Law."

The Bible tells us specifically, we are under obligation to who? No one. The only obligation we have is to love even those who judge you and those who hate you, do this and you will see who is rewarded in the end. I've had to do this many times already in my walk with Christ and being in the church, and it is certainly not easy, but resisting this teaching with a hard and stubborn heart is far worse than loving evil people. Do what God desires and *they* will be on the receiving end of His anger, not you.

117

How to Deal: *With Your Past*

James 4:12 "God is the only law-giver and judge. He alone can save and destroy. Who do you think you are to judge someone else?"
Romans 2:5 "But you have a hard and stubborn heart, and so you are making your own punishment even greater on the Day when God's anger and righteous judgments will be revealed."

Quit judging each other and just do your best to *strengthen* others with the true Word and build others up instead. Look, it's hard enough being a woman, but being a woman who is a believer in Christ? Lord, have mercy…a sister can't even *live!* We need to encourage each other and build each other up, no matter our views or our personal beliefs. Quit tearing each other down! Women, especially Christian women, are always being judged and torn down by the media and by other women, let's not add to that, okay?

Romans 14:19 "So then, we must always aim at those things that bring peace and that help strengthen one another."
Galatians 6:8-10 "If you plant in the field of natural desires, from it you will gather the harvest of death; if you plant in the field of the Spirit, from the Spirit you will gather the harvest of eternal life. So let us not become tired of doing good; for if we do not give up, the time will come when we will reap the harvest. So then, as often as we have the chance, we should do good to everyone, and especially to those who belong to our family in the faith."

Don't Dwell on Choices of the Past

Job 11:13-18 "Put your heart right. Reach out to God. Put away evil and wrong from your home. Then face the world again, firm and courageous. Then all your troubles will fade from your memory. – Your life will be brighter than sunshine at noon, and life's darkest hours will shine like the dawn. You will live secure and full of hope; God will protect you and give you rest."

Put your heart right, love others, and encourage others; we're trying to bring people to salvation, not destruction. If you can get your act right and do good to others, once you come out of this season, even your darkest hours won't seem so bad because you will know that God is on your side, and you will put your trust in Him to get you through it again. And through your journey, remember to love others and to do good to everyone, to build others up in the faith and not tear them down. Do not become tired of doing good, especially to your family in the faith, and you will be blessed for it. You never know what that person may be destined for. God can, and wants to, use anyone and everyone! Even the worst of the worst. Take Saul for example:

Galatians 1:13 "You have been told how I used to live when I was devoted to the Jewish religion, how I persecuted without mercy the church of God and did my best to destroy it."

119

How to Deal: *With Your Past*

Acts 8:3 "Saul tried to destroy the church; going from house to house, he dragged out the believers, both men and women, and threw them into jail."
Acts 9:1 "In the meantime Saul kept up his violent threats of murder against the followers of the Lord."

Saul was the worst of the sinners, but when he was called by Jesus, everything changed. Just one experience with Jesus will change your whole life in ways you would never imagine. Maybe you know someone who was deep in sin and recently had an encounter with the Lord and gave their life to Christ and appears to have had a complete turnaround in their life and you're thinking, *that's got to be too good to be true, there's no way he changed that quickly, this must be another one of his schemes, he's surely up to no good.* Listen to me, no one is too difficult for God to reach in *His* time! And God absolutely can completely turn someone around *that* quickly!

Acts 9:3-5 "As Saul was coming near the city of Damascus, suddenly a light from the sky flashed around him. He fell to the ground and heard a voice saying to him, 'Saul, Saul! Why do you persecute me?' 'Who are you, Lord?' he asked. 'I am Jesus, whom you persecute,' the voice said."
Acts 9:8 "Saul got up from the ground and opened his eyes, but could not see a thing."

Don't Dwell on Choices of the Past

After Saul was called by Jesus, he lost his vision for three days. In your new journey with Christ, you will likely face some struggles like you've never experienced before, as you begin to walk by faith you will literally feel like you are blind and completely lost, but push through, God must test your faith and break you in order to build you back up and use you for something greater. Like Saul, you won't be able to "see" what in the world He is doing! But if you just keep walking with Him by faith, in time it will all make sense. He needs to know you can trust Him, that's faith.

When *Jesus* was ready, He called a man names Ananias into place to step in and place His hands on Saul so he might see again. Those people who knew about Saul's past questioned the Lord about His decision, but He responded,

Acts 9:15-16 "The Lord said to him, 'Go, because I have chosen him to serve Me, to make My name known to Gentiles and kings and to the people of Israel. And I Myself will show him all that he must suffer for My sake."

He doesn't care about your past! He knows that He can use you and make you into a new being, He has that power! Notice how He says, "I myself will show him", as I said before, it is not up to others to punish you, shame or condemn you or show you what God wants, God is more

121

than capable of doing this on His own. That's why relationship with Him is so important; He will show you.

Acts 9:20 "[Saul] went straight to the synagogues and began to preach that Jesus was the Son of God."

Once he received his sight, he went *straight* to start spreading the Word. Like I said, it doesn't take long to turn around and be on fire for God. He couldn't wait to share what he had received. This is exactly how it was for me, you guys. I immediately wanted to share with the world what I had experienced and what the Lord had showed me in hopes that they would receive the same incredible experiences that I was blessed to witness and experience. It was such a blessing to share in Christ's sufferings, because as torturous as the pain was (and still is) that I had to endure, even the smallest amount of peace and blessings I receive now are more than worth the pain in the struggle. There was purpose in it all.

Because of who I *was,* I can relate to a whole different people than, say, my husband, who was raised in the church. I can speak from a different place than a lot of believers. This is something so powerful and fulfilling to me. I'm not just sharing that God is real because that is what I was taught as a child, but because that is my *experience,* despite what I so firmly believed.

Don't Dwell on Choices of the Past

Acts 9:22 "But Saul's preaching became even more powerful, and his proofs that Jesus was the Messiah were so convincing that the Jews who lived in Damascus could not answer him."

A man who had done such horrible things, specifically to the body of Christ, was able to be saved for the glory of God and was able to be used in a way that was greater and more powerful than any other man preaching God's Word; he even ended up writing most of the books in the New Testament! This proves true the scripture,

Matthew 21:42 "The stone which the builders rejected as worthless turned out to be the most important of all."

So, when people ask, "…even addicts?" yes. "…even drug dealers?" yes. "…even murders?" yes. "…even rapists?" yes! Or would you prefer they remain rejected and isolated with their thoughts, never receive rehabilitation, and continue the cycle of abuse? I don't think so. The most worthless stone can absolutely turn out to be the most useful. I thank God He turned Saul around and allowed him the opportunity to write the books he wrote. He had a view and an authority that most didn't.

How to Deal: *With Your Past*

It's okay to share your story, you don't have to hide and be ashamed of your past, you can use your past to become the most important of all! Just don't let it hold you back. Share it as a testimony to help others. Share it with a victorious ending. Don't let others use it against you and don't block what God has in store for you. Allow Him to bless your socks off. Allow Him to use your bad for your good, allow *Him* to write your ending; I promise you it'll be better than anything you could do on your own. You are a beacon of hope for other sinners.

Romans 5:3 "We also boast of our troubles, because we know that trouble produces endurance, endurance brings God's approval, and His approval creates hope. This hope does not disappoint us, for God has poured out His love into our hearts by means of the Holy Spirit, who is God's gift to us."
Zechariah 10:7 "Their descendants will remember this victory and be glad because of what the Lord has done."

Let this lesson be passed down and use your victory to create hope for generations to come. I know it can be hard, some tests are harder to get through and harder to understand than others. Consider Abraham's test; God wanted him to physically go and sacrifice his own son. But he did not question the Lord, and he was blessed because of his willingness, obedience, confidence, and great faith in Him. It was just a test by the way, God didn't actually make him kill his son. In comparison I suppose our little test of leaving everything behind by faith wasn't so big after all.

Matthew 24:13 "But whoever holds out to the end will be saved."

So, stay strong, don't let people get you down about your past, hold out to the end and God will bless you. Not all believers have it all right, but don't let that be a poor reflection on God. People won't always get everything right, sometimes the ones we struggle with most are our own family, but have grace for them, pray for them, guide them through scripture and if the relationship is severed for His sake, the Lord will reward you. Family is precious, but salvation is through Christ alone.

Matthew 19:29 "And everyone who has left houses or brothers or sisters or father or mother or children or fields for My sake, will receive a hundred times more and will be given eternal life."
Acts 4:12 "Salvation is to be found through Him alone; in all the world there is no one else whom God has given who can save us."

I have been run off by "holier than thou" Christians for far too long. I will not let their opinions and judgments hold me back any longer. My salvation depends on it. I know

125

where my salvation comes from, and it is not from any man. God's grace and His mercy are what will carry me through.

Acts 5:29 "We must obey God, not men."
Acts 4:29 "And now, Lord, take notice of the threats they have made, and allow us, Your servants, to speak Your message with all boldness."
Ephesians 1:4 "Even before the world was made, God had already chosen us to be His through our union with Christ, so that we would be holy and without fault before Him."

God was ready for us before we were even born, He chose us, and He waited for the perfect time to call us. He stood by and watched every move we made, every sin we committed, He wants us to repent and be holy and without fault before Him. His mercy is given freely to those who love Him! Claim it for yourself! Repent for your past and better your future; it's never too late!

Romans 9:16 "everything depends, not on what we humans want or do, but only by God's mercy."
2 Corinthians 4:16 "For this reason we never become discouraged. Even though our physical being is gradually decaying, yet our spiritual being is renewed day after day."

Part 2

How to Deal: *With the Present*

Chapter 4

Have Faith

Our journey through this life is intended to be one of faith, not sight. It is the foundation for which you will accomplish and endure what God has placed on your life. Let the Spirit of God lead you. It's going to feel uncomfortable. Don't be surprised if you experience doubt, fear, and insecurity and begin second guessing yourself. You may even get angry or frustrated, it's normal. I wanted to give up *so many times!* Keep stepping. Commit to moving by faith. Push through the hard times. Push through when you cannot see the step in front of you. If you don't just *do* it, you'll never find out if it really is God or not. For me, I *had* to know for myself, that He is who He says He is. Don't take my word for it, find out for yourself! You have been called to more than a life of comfort, ease, safety, and security. We are invited into the faith adventure with Jesus. It is an invitation; we choose whether to accept or deny. My recommendation, choose faith.

Faith is the first and most important step in dealing with your present situations; it all starts with faith. We are *saved* by faith in *Him*. In order to be in right standing with God and receive His reward and blessings, you've got to have faith which allows you to believe in His power at work in your life, to believe that your situation will turn around. Even if it sounds crazy and far beyond your reach, nothing is out of God's reach!

At that moment of activating your faith God will activate His favor. I had been told time and time again, this time by Smith Wigglesworth's great granddaughter, Lilian DeFin, that the blessings I was asking and believing God for were being held up in the fact that my boyfriend (now husband) and I, were not yet married. I was fearful, I never in my life had a desire to be married and certainly not under these uncertain conditions, but at some point, I had to step by faith believing that God would bless our union when we came into alignment and stopped living in sin against His will and His Word. So, I stepped, blindly, by faith. We got married quickly after that and the Lord has blessed us ever since. Every time we step by faith, we see the blessing of the Lord follow.

How to Deal: *With the Present*

Do you believe in God? Then you've got to believe that God's Word is true yesterday, today and forever, and that His promises are true, and you can claim them for yourself. Otherwise, what are you doing?? Try Him, He is good to keep His Word!

Romans 1:17 "For the gospel reveals how God puts people right with Himself: it is through faith from beginning to end."
Hebrews 11:6 "No one can please God without faith, for whoever comes to God must have faith that God exists and rewards those who seek Him."

So how do you prove your faith? You've got to confess with your mouth out loud that Jesus Christ is your Lord and Savior and that He died for your sins and was raised again. If you truly believe that and you confess it with your mouth, you are saved!

Romans 10:9-11 "If you confess that Jesus is Lord and believe that God raised Him from death, you will be saved. For it is by our faith that we are put right with God; it is by our confession that we are saved. The scripture says, 'Whoever believes in Him will not be disappointed.'"

Now, you might think, "Well, God knows my heart, He knows that I believe those things. God knows my thoughts. I'm pretty sure I've said that before. It's not that serious." Well, let's take a look at how important your confession really is…the Bible says:

Matthew 10:32 "Those who <u>declare publicly</u> that they belong to Me, I will do the same for them before my Father in Heaven."
Philippians 2:11 "and all will <u>openly proclaim</u> that Jesus Christ is Lord, to the glory of God the Father."
1 John 2:23 "For those who reject the Son reject also the Father; those who accept the Son have the Father also."
1 John 4:15 "<u>If we declare</u> that Jesus is the Son of God, we live in union with God and God lives in union with us."
Matthew 16:16 "Simon Peter answered, 'You are the Messiah, the Son of the living God.'"
John 6:69 "And now we believe and know that You are the Holy One who has come from God."

How to Deal: *With the Present*

Your confession is more than a feeling, it's more than a thought; your faith and confession is the only way to get in right standing with God. Not even doing what's right can get you in right standing with God. This is good news for us as believers, but for our loved ones who are not where we are in our relationship with Christ just yet, but are still good people, this is the saddest news of all.

My mom was not a believer, to my knowledge, but the absolute best, most "godly" person I had ever known. She naturally abided by the Law of Love more than any Christian I had ever seen, yet to my knowledge, was not saved. I thank God, though, that she since has developed her own relationship with Him, because I knew that as good as she is, it would not get her into Heaven, and the thought of that was absolutely devastating. Jesus is the only way, and it is your faith confession that will save your eternal soul.

One big mistake that a lot of believers make is thinking there's anything we can do to deserve or earn God's blessings, healing, grace, mercy, and favor. The truth is we are all sinners; there is nothing we can ever *do* to deserve *anything* from God. We just don't deserve it! None of us are good enough, none of us are holy enough.

Have Faith

Galatians 5:4 "Those of you who try to be put right with God by obeying the Law have cut yourselves off from Christ. You are outside God's grace."
Romans 3:28 "For we conclude that a person is put right with God only through faith, and not by doing what the Law commands."

Your good acts, your obedience to the Law, praying, fasting, and tithing; although these are all good and important, none of these things, without faith, will get God to move in your life! None of them will get you to Heaven. You can go your whole life having never murdered anyone, and that's great, no doubt, but that doesn't mean you're saved. You can be the meanest, rudest, nastiest, law-breaking, sinful, scheming, lousy person who believes in God and received Jesus Christ and will get into Heaven, while the nicest, sweetest, kindest, most selfless soul you have ever met who is not a believer and has not accepted Christ, unfortunately will not get to Heaven. It's not about kindness or works, it's all about faith.

Now, that is an extreme example, because if you are a believer, surely you should be striving to be kind and do good, however humans are human, and that isn't always the case; but God's grace is not real grace if you are only given what you *deserve* or *earn*. You've got to have faith first. You've got to believe when it's hard, you've got to believe when it seems impossible, you've got to believe that God IS MAKING a way; not based on your circumstances, but in spite of your circumstances. Believe in Him despite the facts.

Proverbs 3:5 "Trust in the Lord with all your heart. Never rely on what you think you know."

YOU DON'T KNOW WHAT GOD IS ABOUT TO DO WITH YOUR SITUATION! You don't! Being still somewhat new in my faith walk, I keep catching myself thinking, *well, I've tried that before and I failed, I fell flat on my face, that doesn't work*...but then I have to catch myself and realize, I've never tried it *with Him!* There's a difference. Doing it on your own, you can absolutely fail, one hundred percent. But try it again, *with Him.* If it's what He's promised you, this time *will* be different! Don't think that just because you've seen this movie play out before, you know what the ending is going to be. You are just one bad thought away from getting the junk you're expecting. CHANGE YOUR THINKING!

What is it going to hurt you to actually expect good things for yourself? You might get let down? Guess what, God is not the men you're used to, He is not the friend you're used to, and thank God for me, He is not the father you're used to. I had such a hard time coming to God with anything for *so long* because my dad used to complain that I

134

only ever contacted him when I needed something, well duh! Welcome to raising a teenager. But God is different.

It's so funny because I think of how I used to pray, "God, I know You're so busy, but if You just answer this *one* prayer, I swear I'll never ask You for anything again!" Let me say this loud and clear, *THAT'S NOT WHAT HE WANTS!!* Man, He is *so much better* than we can even imagine. Take it to Him, whatever it is, He *wants* you to call on Him; ask Him! God will not let you down. You might not understand the whole process, it might not happen at the exact time or exact way you'd like it to or expect it to, but ultimately, God will come through. His timing is perfect. He will not let you down! You can rest in Him. Rest in His Word.

Isaiah 60:22 "At the right time, I, the Lord, will make it happen."
Romans 5:1 "Now that we have been put right with God through faith, we have peace with God through our Lord Jesus Christ."

He will first give you the peace to endure the process until the day His blessings come. That may not seem like a big deal now, but I can tell you from my own experience, it's better to go through trials with His perfect peace than without it, and this peace is almost better than the blessing itself! I mean, I was never this peaceful and content even when I had everything I thought I needed and wanted!

135

How to Deal: *With the Present*

Someone asked me recently, why people who don't even believe in God can be so successful and fulfilled. My response was, as someone who has been successful and had legitimately everything I could have wanted, it appeared to people on the outside that I was a "nonbeliever" who was successful and fulfilled, but in reality, I was *so empty*.

I was living on the beach in a *beautiful* three-story home, I had a man who was *crazy* about me. I didn't work. My closet was full, and my man would take me shopping almost daily to the point I was irritated with the malls because I already owned everything they had that I wanted. I never once used my kitchen because we ate out at five-star restaurants for every meal, every day. But after all that, I would come home and feel so empty, waiting for the next thing to come entertain me.

The point is, you can look at someone and think they have it all when really, they are more empty than you could ever imagine. That is why you see so many rich and famous people take their own lives. It is not all that it seems to be. There is a void that we all have that can *only* be filled by our Creator. I had everything, yet I was always looking for what's next; now I have seemingly nothing, and I'm just enjoying what is! I am full. I am blessed. I have been on both sides, and while it is *wonderful* to be able to pay your bills without sacrificing a meal, it is far more fulfilling to be filled with the love of God. You have my word. I'm not lying, I promise you!

Jesus made it so easy for us, He *wants* us to *rest* in Him. Many people still think we must *do this* or *don't do that* in order to please God and get what we want; some people still quote the Law of Moses or the Ten Commandments in an attempt to condemn people for living wrong, and while the Bible says you should still acknowledge the Law, it is important to know that Jesus came and brought with Him a new Law.

James 1:25 "But if you look closely into the perfect law that sets people free, and keep on paying attention to it and do not simply listen and then forget it, but put it into practice – you will be blessed by God in what you do."

The Law of Moses or the Ten Commandments will keep you blessed, because there is wisdom in it. I think most would agree it is wise to not murder; however, it is not the Law of the Old Testament that we must concern ourselves with, it is the Perfect Law of Liberty, which is the Law of Love that Jesus came to teach and fulfill.

137

How to Deal: *With the Present*

Actions, whether good or bad, are not a requirement for God's love, mercy, grace, or salvation; He loves us all equally and gives to all freely. The point is, the Law is good to keep us in sync, but Jesus came to fulfill the Law and save us by His grace, not our own abilities. It's about balance! But if we think that we must be good and do good and obey the Law to perfection, then that would mean Jesus' sacrifice on our behalf wasn't good enough, and that is simply not true. We strive for greatness, but rest in His mercy, His grace, and His love.

Have faith and continue to love, and God will bless you. Too often I hear believers say, "If it is God's will, I'll be blessed financially" and continue to live a life just getting by and be okay with it! Bro! Get in the Word! Know it for yourself! Don't keep repeating these phrases you've heard in the church. You're speaking your own failure without even knowing it!

God doesn't want you to be broke and struggle just to get by. He wants to prosper you! What good father wants to see their beloved child struggle through life? No! He wants to bless you with the things you hope for, unbelievable miracles and blessings that you cannot even imagine! All you have to do is have faith; believe it's true and receive the blessings!

Have Faith

Get ready. I mean really, get ready! If someone were to write you a million dollar check right now, would you be ready to receive it? Would you know what to do with it? Most people think they do, but just look at many of the past lottery winners and where they are now. Most of them didn't make it last. You've got to know more than just what you're going to spend it on. You've got to prepare the knowledge to know how to invest it!

Give Him something to work with; if you have a business or product idea but think, *Who am I? I can't start a business. I don't have the resources.* Well, that may be true, but if you have it prepared and give it to God and give Him something to work with, He can step in, open doors, and *make* it successful. Prepare your business plan. Get ready! I have absolutely *zero* faith in myself to make this book anything at all, but I've got about a mustard seed worth to put in the effort and see what He can do with it, so here goes my part.

If He restores your health, are you going to use your testimony to reach others? This season was hard, but how can you use it to impact and encourage someone else's life? Decide now how you're going to use your struggle to help others, and God will bless that! Nobody wants weight loss advice from someone who's always been skinny. Nobody wants sobriety advice from someone who's never been through addiction. Use what you've got! This test of faith is your testimony! He *wants* to bless you! You've just got to be ready to allow Him to!

Jeremiah 29:11 "I alone know the plans I have for you, plans to bring you prosperity and not disaster, plans to bring about the future you hope for."

Sometimes it's easy to lose your faith when you don't understand what's going on and why, when we think that God has just forgotten about us. One of the reasons God sends us through these trials is to test our faith. Even if it does happen to be a test from the devil, we know nothing happens without God's approval.

Amos 3:6 "Does disaster strike a city unless the Lord sends it?"
Isaiah 45:7 "I form light and create darkness, I make well-being and create calamity, I am the Lord, who does all these things."

Yes, that's God's Word! Everything that happens, good or terribly bad, is either sent or allowed by God Himself; and this is where most people get very upset with God, but God is good, and with Him in control, He *will* turn it around for your good. So don't stress or worry even when you're going through hard times. God knows, and He wouldn't send or allow anything you couldn't handle or anything He's not prepared to bring you out of and reward you for. Remain close to Him, and He will bring you through.

1 Peter 1:6-7 "Be glad about this, even though it may now be necessary for you to be sad for a while because of the many kinds of trials you suffer. Their purpose is to prove that your faith is genuine. Even gold, which can be destroyed, is tested by fire; and so your faith, which is much more precious than gold, must also be tested, so that it may endure."

God is the reason for all things; nothing is done without His say so. But although it may bring you a lot of suffering, He wants you to be glad! The fact that He asks us to be glad about this is because He wants to see that you have faith in Him to turn it around for your good, even while you're in the mess, and He will! He is refining us in the fire like gold, not because He hates us but *because* we are valuable. Prove through these trials that your faith is genuine, and He will take you places you couldn't even *dream* of.

If faith was always easy, it wouldn't take faith. He wants you to trust Him through the darkness and give Him all the glory for the turn around. He wants you to turn and focus all your attention on Him throughout the process and the Bible says that if you are faithful, He will give you life as your prize of victory!

How to Deal: *With the Present*

Revelation 2:9-10 "I know your troubles; I know that you are poor — but really you are rich! I know the evil things said against you by those who claim to be Jews but are not; they are a group that belongs to Satan! Don't be afraid of anything you are about to suffer. Listen! The devil will put you to the test by having some of you thrown into prison, and your troubles will last ten days. Be faithful to Me, even if it means death, and I will give you life as your prize of victory."

This scripture is a perfect example of speaking faith during trials, "I know that you are poor — but really you are rich!" Now, how can you be poor and rich at the same time? You may not have physical money right now but having access to the Lord's blessings will get you more than money could buy!

We have the wrong idea of wealth. We live in a time where people will sell eternity for a couple bucks for today. They will risk their future by quarreling, stealing, killing, and scheming for money, not realizing there is a prize far greater than money, which is eternal. Money is great, we need it to survive, but it doesn't last.

He tells us not to worry about anything you are about to suffer but be faithful to Him and He will give you *your* prize of victory. You don't have to quarrel, steal, kill or scheme for it, the prize is already yours! He has paid for it all! It already belongs to you! But you must know what is yours so you can claim it; all you have to do is remain faithful and claim what has already been promised to you! It's not on layaway, it's already been paid for! Pick up your gift!

The promises of God and access to His miracles is the greatest blessing you could receive, and all it takes is faith. The Bible speaks a lot about faith; it is the foundation for everything. Healings were and are still done through faith. Just look at some of the miracle healings that Jesus performed; most of them were based heavily on the people's faith.

Acts 14:9 "He sat there and listened to Paul's words. Paul saw that he **believed** *and could be healed, so he [healed him]."*

Luke 7:50 "But Jesus said to the woman, 'Your **faith** *has saved you; go in peace.'"*

Luke 8:50 "But Jesus heard it and said to Jairus, 'Don't be afraid; only **believe**, *and she will be well.'"*

Luke 18:42 "Jesus said to him, 'Then see! Your **faith** *has made you well.'"*

John 11:40 "Jesus said to her, 'Didn't I tell you that you would see God's glory if you **believed**?'"*

How to Deal: *With the Present*

Matthew 15:28 "So Jesus answered her, 'You are a woman of great **faith***! What you want will be done for you.' And at that very moment her daughter was healed."*
Matthew 8:13 "Then Jesus said to the officer, 'Go home, and what you **believe** *will be done for you."*
Matthew 9:22 "Jesus turned around and saw her, and said, 'Courage, My daughter! Your **faith** *has made you well.' At that very moment the women became well."*
Matthew 9:28-29 "'Do you **believe** *that I can heal you' 'Yes, Sir!' they answered. Then Jesus touched their eyes and said, 'Let it happen, then,* just as you **believe***!' – and their sight was restored."*

Why are so many great big miracles seen overseas and with new believers, yet experienced Christians will wait on a little puny miracle for years? Maybe it's not the time, but could it be that we've lost our child-like faith in God's healing power? It is by *our* faith that we receive. Don't let years of Christianity harden your faith. Remember the zeal you had as a new believer. Anything was possible! Believe in His power like your faith is all you have, as if it's your only hope.

Often, nonbelievers face hard times, hit rock bottom and only then do they have no choice but to look up, and finally turn to God for help and receive His answer – a way out of an impossible place. That's what it was for me. So why do we as believers often want to turn *away* from God the minute we face difficulties, as if it's His fault? Why is He the *answer* to unbelievers and the *cause* to those who "believe"? Strengthen your faith!

"Let it happen, then, just as you believe!" All it takes is the faith the size of a mustard seed for it to happen, but that doesn't mean your faith has to stay small. If your faith is small, your reward will be small, "just as you believe". If you believe for just a little healing, you will receive just a little healing, "just as you believe". If you're believing for a just-getting-by financial increase, don't be surprised when that's all you get! Believe for big! God can do it! Believe that you can heal your loved ones by the authority in your voice! You have that same power to heal and perform miracles as Jesus and His disciples did, through Christ. But again, it takes *faith* to activate it.

Matthew 17:20 "'It was because you did not have enough faith,' answered Jesus. 'I assure you that if you have faith as big as a mustard seed, you can say to this hill, 'Go from here to there!' and it will go. You could do anything!'"
Matthew 21:21-22 "'I assure you that if you believe and do not doubt, you will be able to do what I have done to this fig tree. And not only this, but you will even be able to say to this hill, 'Get up and throw yourself in the sea,' and it will. If you believe, you will receive whatever you ask for in prayer."

How to Deal: *With the Present*

Use your God given authority! Faith along with the Holy Spirit (which you receive by faith) gives you access to perform these miracles and ultimately do God's work. Life itself will become much easier if you allow the Holy Spirit to guide you in all that you do.

Galatians 3:14 "Christ [became a curse for us] in order that the blessing which God promised Abraham might be given to the Gentiles by means of Christ Jesus, so that through faith we might receive the Spirit promised by God."

I would like to suggest getting in a church that teaches about the Holy Spirit. If your church shies away from Spirit teaching…I'm just saying…it's scriptural. That's where your daily comfort comes from. He is the Comforter! That's where your hope comes from! That's where your strength and power come from! That's where your wisdom comes from. It is *Him* within *you!* Know Him, accept Him, praise Him! Don't leave Him out! He's not weird! He is fully God; He is God in you!

Romans 15:13 "May God, the source of hope, fill you with all joy and peace by means of your faith in Him, so that your hope will continue to grow by the power of the Holy Spirit."

146

Have Faith

Ephesians 3:20 "To him who by means of His power working in us is able to do so much more than we can ever ask for, or even think of."

The Holy Spirit, in us, is able to do so much more than we could even *think* of! He may lead you into some uncomfortable places or situations, but He's got to prepare you for the greater thing He has in store for you. He needs to make you uncomfortable in order to push you out of a place you've mistaken as comfort, and into a greater place of purpose! But God will not give you whatever you want if you are not prepared. You've got to endure some hard times and learn some lessons the hard way and prove that you can handle the great things He wants to give you. Just look at Jesus:

Mark 1:12 "At once the Spirit made [Jesus] go into the wilderness, where He stayed forty days, being tempted by Satan. Wild animals were there also, but angels came and helped Him."

Now, it doesn't say that *Satan* led Jesus into the desert, the Holy Spirit took Jesus through some hard times in the desert in order to teach Him and so He could prove that He was prepared to face temptation and do what God had Him to do. You. Will. Be. Tempted! Expect it! But push through. Focus on the end. Even if you slip up, get back on and see it to the victorious end, and the Holy Spirit in you will give you life.

Romans 8:11 "If the Spirit of God, who raised Jesus from death, lives in you, then He who raised Christ from death will also give life to your mortal bodies by the presence of His Spirit in you."

I'll get more into our power in the Holy Spirit a bit later, but notice, "so that through *faith* we might receive the *Spirit* promised by God…" The Holy Spirit is the means by which we are able to use the power within us and to receive His blessings. Are y'all even aware of the blessings that belong to you?!

"Abraham's promise"

Deuteronomy 28:2-14 "Obey the Lord your God and <u>all</u> these blessings will be yours:

The Lord will bless your towns and your fields.

The Lord will bless you with many children, with abundant crops, and with many cattle and sheep.

The Lord will bless your grain crops and the food you prepare from them.

The Lord will bless <u>everything</u> you do.

The Lord will defeat your enemies when they attack you. They will attack from one direction, but they will run from you in all directions.

Have Faith

The Lord your God will bless your work and fill your barns with grain.
He will bless you in the land that He is giving you.
If you obey the Lord your God and do everything He commands, He will
make you His own people, as He has promised. Then all the peoples on
earth will see that the Lord has chosen you to be His own people, and
they will be afraid of you. The Lord will give you many children, many
cattle, and abundant crops in the land that He promised your ancestors
to give you. He will send rain in season from His rich storehouse in the
sky and bless all your work, so that you will lend to many nations, but
you will not have to borrow from any. The Lord your God will make
you the leader among the nations and not a follower; you will always
prosper and never fail if you obey faithfully all His commands that I am
giving you today."

People might argue that this was just an Old Testament promise, but it is still talked about and promised in the New Testament as well. Is this the kind of blessing you've been after? Do you need your enemies to be defeated and to run from you in all directions? Have you been praying for the Lord to bless you in everything you do? Do you want Him to bless your work? Of course, you do! Maybe you have been praying and hoping for children, you need to first have faith!

Do not speak defeat over your life, no matter what it looks like, no matter what the doctors said. Even down to a minor cold! People always say, "I think I'm catching a cold."

149

No! Speak health! "I am a child of God; I declare healing over my body. I rebuke any harmful virus, germ, bacteria, and disease in my body the Name of Jesus it must go!" Speak it, believe it, and receive it! Your faith will *guarantee* God's promise to come to pass. God's love is unconditional; His blessings, however, are not. You must have faith to receive His promise!!

*Romans 4:16 "And so the promise was based on **faith**, in order that the promise should be <u>guaranteed</u> as God's free gift to all of Abraham's descendants — not just to those who obey the law, but also to those who **believe** as Abraham did. For Abraham is the spiritual father of us all."*

Galatians 3:29 "If you belong to Christ, then you are the descendants of Abraham and will receive what God has promised."

But it's not enough just to *say* you have faith, your actions have to prove it. I mean, think about it; someone can say they love you, but until they show it in their actions, do you really believe them? If someone says they'll be there for you but never shows up, do those words do you any good?

James 2:14 "My friends, what good is it for one of you to say that you have faith if your actions do not prove it? Can that faith save you?"

James 2:17 "So it is with faith: if it is alone and includes no actions, then it is dead."

Have Faith

Before you can be healed, you've got to believe that you can and will be healed and plan for a long and healthy life, God willing. Before your situation can change, you've got to believe that your situation can change and prepare as if you knew it were coming now, today, God willing. Believe it in your heart, believe it in your spirit, speak it with your mouth and act on it! Take actions that seem impossible, fearlessly knowing that God is on your side.

No matter what you're going through, no matter what it looks like, no matter how big your dreams are, you've got to believe that you are in God's hands, and He will never leave you nor forsake you. And if it turns out that God's plan is to take you home just know, to be with the Lord *is not a bad thing!* Trust and believe that He knows your time. Trust that He has a greater picture in mind and count on Him to get you through, regardless of your understanding.

Hebrews 11:1 "To have faith is to be sure of the things we hope for, to be certain of the things we cannot see."
Habakkuk 1:5 "Keep watching — and you will be astonished at what you see. I am going to do something that you will not believe when you hear about it."

How to Deal: *With the Present*

I've heard so many people speak down about their dreams like they can't achieve them. Well, that may be true – without God. But if you've got God on your side, nothing is impossible! "Well, I'd really like to be able to buy my mom a house. I'd really like to be out of debt, but I know that's not realistic for me. I don't make enough money, I'm too far in debt, my parents have always struggled, I'm not smart enough to become rich or successful." Look, it's got nothing to do with you! You can't do anything without God anyway, so get over yourself! How powerful is your God? How much faith do you have in Him? Can He do it? God is no respecter of persons; He doesn't care who you are or what you're capable of!

Acts 10:34 "God is no respecter of persons." KJV

"I'd love to be healthy again. I wish I could have children. I wish I had longer to live, I'd do so much more, but the doctors said…" but what has God said? Won't He do it? If you believe it, not only will He heal you, He will heal you better than before. If you believe it, not only will He prosper you, He will prosper you with more than you even asked for or imagined!

On the day when He acts it will be even greater than what you had been believing for. That's how good He is! If you have faith for one thing and you are sure that He will make it happen, He won't just provide what you're asking for, He will *exceed* it!

Ephesians 3:20 "Now unto Him that is able to do exceeding abundantly above all that we ask or think, according to the power that worketh in us," KJV

Take Job for example, sure, God allowed Satan to tempt him, Satan even harmed Job's body, but when all was said and done Job kept the faith, and when he was ready to receive God's blessings, God restored his skin and body *better* than before.

Job 2:7 "Then Satan left the Lord's presence and made sores break out all over Job's body."
Job 33:25 "His flesh shall be fresher than a child's: he shall return to the days of his youth." KJV

God gives back better than before. It may not happen exactly when you want it or when you expect it, but you've got to trust His timing. Don't get discouraged if it doesn't happen when you want it to or when you think it should. If God told you exactly when it would happen or made everything happen right away when you asked, it wouldn't take faith! But if God made you a promise, you can be sure He *will* make it happen.

Galatians 6:9 "And let us not grow weary while doing good, for in due season we shall reap if we do not lose heart." NKJV

So do good and speak greatness and victory! Change the channel of negative thoughts and don't let them take root in your spirit; that's the enemy. The father of lies will tell you that it's never going to happen for you. He will plant those lies in your mind and fill you with doubt. The serpent didn't tempt Adam and Eve by convincing them to steal, kill and destroy, He simply convinced them to question God. Who will you trust? God is not the only spiritual father with influence over you; Satan is the father of the earth. You have a choice on whose voice you will allow to influence you. But if you believe the lies of doubt, you are listening to the wrong father!

Ephesians 2:2 "You used to live in sin, just like the rest of the world, obeying the devil – the commander of the powers in the unseen world. He is the spirit at work in the hearts of those who refuse to obey God."
John 8:44-47 "You are the children of your father, the devil, and you want to follow your father's desires. From the very beginning he was a murderer and has never been on the side of the truth, because there is no truth in him. When he tells a lie, he is only doing what is natural to

him, because he is a liar and the father of all lies. But I tell the truth, and that is why you do not believe me. Which one of you can prove that I am guilty of sin? If I tell the truth, then why do you not believe me? He who comes from God listens to God's words. You, however, are not from God, and that is why you will not listen."

Don't believe his lies! Does God say He wants you sick or your child sick and to never get better? No. Does God say He wants your children to be rebellious and far from Him? No. Does God's Word say He wants you to be financially poor and struggle through life? No! Does God tell you that you will never have children? No.

You want to see an example of big faith gone wrong? Look at Sarai, she thought she would never have children and even when God promised she would, she tried to get ahead of God's timing by insisting that Abram conceive the promised child with their servant, Hagar; but God didn't need her help or intervention, and He doesn't need ours. In *His* time, God still fulfilled His promise to Sarai, as He said He would.

Genesis 15:5-6 "Look at the sky and try to count the stars; you will have as many descendants as that. Abram put his <u>trust</u> in the Lord, and because of this the Lord was pleased with him and accepted him."

How to Deal: *With the Present*

This was a big promise to have faith for, but Abram trusted the Lord, and *because* of this, the Lord was pleased with him and accepted him. Sarai, however, heard this promise and laughed! She was ninety years old and no longer had a menstrual cycle! Any doctor these days would tell her it was impossible to conceive a child. Sarai became impatient in God's timing and decided to give up on her faith in God's promise and took matters into her own hands.

Genesis 16:2 "and so [Sarai] said to Abram, 'The Lord has kept me from having children. Why don't you sleep with my slave? Perhaps she can have a child for me.' Abram agreed with what Sarai said."
Genesis 17:19 "But God said, 'No. Your wife Sarah will bear you a son and you will name him Isaac.'"

Within this time, God had told Abram he will now be called Abraham and Sarai will now be called Sarah. This just shows how God will have to change you before He will release His blessings upon you. There's purpose in the "waiting period". Don't resist the change. He promised Abraham once again that he would have a child by his wife, Sarah.

Genesis 18:13-14 "Then the Lord asked Abraham, 'Why did Sarah laugh and say, 'Can I really have a child when I am so old?' Is anything too hard for the Lord?'"

Have Faith

Genesis 21:1-2 "The Lord blessed Sarah, as He had promised, and she became pregnant and bore a son to Abraham when he was old. The boy was born at the time God had said he would be born."
Hebrews 11:11 "It was faith that made Abraham able to become a father, even though he was too old and Sarah herself could not have children. He trusted God to keep His promise."

It doesn't matter how impossible it may seem to you, if God said it, He doesn't need your help. You don't need to manipulate and try to figure it out *for* Him, He will bring it to pass. Don't become impatient and manipulate the situation in an attempt to "help God out" because the promise seems impossible. Don't turn to what is familiar or makes logical sense because you don't think God is big enough to keep His promise without your measly help. He's got something so much greater for you! Sarah did this and caused a lot of pain and suffering for a lot of people, including herself.

Even Rebekah struggled with infertility for 20 years, they prayed and finally, in God's time, He blessed her with twins! Unlike Sarah, she didn't become impatient in the process, and in return for her *patience* and *faith* she earned a *double* blessing!

How to Deal: *With the Present*

Genesis 25:21 & 24 "Because Rebecca had no children, Isaac prayed to the Lord for her. The Lord answered his prayer, and Rebecca became pregnant."
24 "The time came for her to give birth, and she had twin sons."

Isaac was forty years old when he married Rebekah and he was sixty years old by the time she gave birth, so after twenty years of infertility, she was finally able to conceive, and had TWINS! I've seen couples complain and get discouraged that they've been trying to get pregnant for *one year* with no results, imagine having the faith to wait TWENTY YEARS! But God's timing is God's timing; we've got to be patient and trust it. If God worked according to our time and demands, He'd be our employee, not the Lord of our lives. His timing is in our best interest. Our God is MORE than enough! He will repay you DOUBLE for your faith through trouble! There are so many other examples of infertility in the Bible that end in victory.

Psalm 113:9 "Into the home of the childless bride, He sends children who are, for her, a cause of happiness beyond measure."

If God has promised it to you, then don't worry about it! Keep your faith in Him strong over all doubt and attack of the enemy and in His time, He will be sure to bless you. He is our provider; God is the giver of all things.

Have Faith

Romans 11:36 "For from Him and through Him and for Him are all things. To Him be the glory forever! Amen." NIV

Everything comes from Him, He is our source, our provider. He is a big God, He doesn't need our intervention, He can provide us with all things so long as we remain in Him. He knows what we need, and it is His desire to provide it. Focus on Him and He will focus on you.

Matthew 6:31-33 "So do not start worrying: 'Where will my food come from? or my drink? or my clothes?' Your Father in Heaven knows that you need all these things. Instead, be concerned above everything else with the Kingdom of God and with what He requires of you, and He will provide you with all these other things."

Don't sweat the small stuff. *If* you've got faith to rest in Him and focus your energy on doing good for the Kingdom of God, you won't need to worry about things like food, clothes, and the daily things you need to survive. God will bring you the victory. He doesn't need you to figure it all out, He only asks you to trust that He already has.

Even if your faith slips up along the way, God is good! Continue to speak your victory over your situation, even if it is not here yet. You *will* rise again!

How to Deal: *With the Present*

Micah 7:8-9 "Our enemies have no reason to gloat over us. We have fallen, but we will rise again. We are in darkness now, but the Lord will give us light. We have sinned against the Lord, so now we must endure His anger for a while. But in the end He will defend us and right the wrongs that have been done to us. He will bring us out to the light; we will live to see Him save us."

How good is God? This scripture just said we have sinned against God so we must endure His anger for a while, but He will defend us...*even though we sinned against Him!* And He will right the wrongs done to us...even though we really brought it upon ourselves. It doesn't say we *might* rise again, and He *might* give us light, He *might* defend us, no! He *will* do it! Speak victory over your situation everyday with great confidence! He will restore what you yourself have destroyed. He will! And He always builds it back better.

Micah 7:11 "the time to rebuild the city walls is coming. At that time your territory will be enlarged."

Have faith that when God is ready to rebuild your situation, He will rebuild it bigger and better than it was before; that's God's way! He will restore to you more than you lost! He will reward you so greatly that you may even forget the pain you went through, as though it never happened.

Zechariah 10:6 "I will have compassion on them and bring them back home. They will be as though I had never rejected them. I am the Lord their God; I will answer their prayers."

You will feel His love so greatly that you will forget ever questioning if He had forgotten about you, you will regret ever turning away from Him. Your faith will come out so much stronger that in your next trial, you won't ever have to question if God is on your side or if He's ever going to show up. You will know by faith that He is *always* with you, and He will never leave your side and your enemies cannot defeat you.

Malachi 4:3 "On the day when I act, you will overcome the wicked, and they will be like dust under your feet."
Zechariah 9:11-12 "The Lord says, 'Because of My covenant with you that was sealed by the blood of sacrifices, I will set your people free — free from the waterless pit of exile. Return, you exiles who now have hope; return to your place of safety. Now I tell you that I will repay you twice over with blessing for all you have suffered.'"

How great is that?! If you will just endure this season and *learn* and don't look back on what *was,* you will end up with *double* what you ever had before!! So have faith in God, go through struggles without fear, and continue to do good until the day He comes to repay you.

Daniel 10:19 "God loves you, so don't let anything worry you or frighten you."
1 Thessalonians 3:3 "You yourselves know that such persecutions are part of God's will for us."

God's will for us is always good, so if trials are God's will for us, don't be worried or frightened, there is a very good reason for it. Consider these trials a blessing, the bigger the trial, the more you'll learn and the bigger the blessing. It strengthens your faith, builds your endurance, and gives you new perspective and fresh revelation.

James 1:2-4 "My friends, consider yourselves fortunate when all kinds of trials come your way, for you know that when your faith succeeds in facing such trials, the result is the ability to endure. Make sure that your endurance carries you all the way without failing, so that you may be perfect and complete, lacking nothing."

"When your *faith* succeeds...you will be *perfect*, lacking *nothing*!" What!? JUST TRY IT! It won't hurt. Go all in! Rest in Him and see how your life turns around. He will reward you for your faithfulness in trials.

Have Faith

James 1:12 "Happy are those who remain faithful under trials, because when they succeed in passing such a test, they will receive as their reward the life which God has promised to those who love Him."

The trials are not promised to last only ten days or seven months, you don't know how long you will have to remain faithful through the trial, but you surely don't want to quit when you're right around the corner from the blessing. Don't compromise for the counterfeit. Hold on, don't let doubt slip in, no matter what may come your way. We all fall into the valley of doubt, it's in our human nature; but it's how you respond to it that's going to make or break you. Do. Not. Settle. For. Less.

*Matthew 14:28-31 "Then Peter spoke up. 'Lord, if it is really You, order me to come out on the water to You.' 'Come!' answered Jesus. So Peter got out of the boat and started walking on the water to Jesus. But when he noticed the strong wind, **he was afraid** and **started to sink** down in the water. 'Save me, Lord!' he cried. At once Jesus reached out and grabbed hold of him and said, 'What little **faith** you have! Why did you doubt?'"*

Peter was already walking on top of the water; he saw that Jesus was able and keeping him afloat! He *knew* Jesus had him. Sometimes it can be like that. We know we are floating but still question the wind. It is your lack of faith that will cause you to sink when He's already keeping you up. Peter let the wind frighten him before he even started to sink! It was his lack of faith through the scary times that made him sink, not the wind itself.

Embrace the storms, learn all that you can, look at life through a new lens! Everything is an experience with purpose. Let it build your faith, then use your faith at all times, in all ways, not just in your life but to encourage others and build them up as well. You never know who is watching, and you never know who is listening. It's a way of life! Your story of faith, like mine, can be used to help others and vice versa.

Romans 1:12 "What I mean is that both you and I will be helped at the same time, you by my faith and I by yours."

Chapter 5

Repent, Forgive, and Pray!

As a new believer, I had a really hard time figuring out how to pray. Not about what to say or how to format a prayer or anything like that, but I just wasn't *feeling* it. I felt like I was talking to empty space, and nobody was listening. It felt silly, impersonal, and honestly, I felt like I was wasting my time. It just didn't feel real to me. I would get exhausted at just the thought of praying; but I knew I couldn't let the intimidation keep me from prayer.

Prayer is so important for your relationship with God; imagine having a relationship with a spouse but you never talk to them. There's no way for you to grow together and you can never become close. So, while there is no one correct way to pray, I will share some tips that helped me overcome the intimidation of prayer and go in and feel the intimacy with the Lord in my prayer time.

When I get into prayer, the first thing I want to do is just focus on Him, call Him in. Thank Him for His goodness. Praise Him for who He is to me. Praise Him for what He's already done and what He's about to do in my life. I think about my 12-year-old daughter, she knows this concept very well; every time she really wants something, she will approach me with compliments and back rubs. Although I know there is a motive and an ask right around the corner, it makes it harder to say no when she's showing me her appreciation for my very existence (and working out week old knots in my back).

I approach God that same way, not just saying, "Alright God, I need a million dollars, fix my life!" No, first think of Him. In praising Him, you will be reminded, yourself, of His goodness and willingness to provide those things you want from Him. This is actually scriptural, too. When God would send people into battle, He would send Judah in first. The meaning of the name Judah is praise. This is symbolic of God's order. If you lead with praise, He will bring you the victory in your battle.

Repent, Forgive, & Pray!

Even if you can't imagine anything good happening, even if you can't think of anything He's done for you, be bold enough to praise Him for what He *can* do, or what He's done for others, believing that He can do it for you, too! Even if you don't feel worthy of His goodness, praise Him for His *mercy* to be good to you! He is so good that no matter what you're going through, no matter what you've done, regardless of what you think or feel, He is always good, always loving and always worthy of praise! He is *for you!*

Habakkuk 3:2 "O Lord, I have heard of what You have done, and I am filled with awe. Now do again in our times the great deeds You used to do. Be merciful, even when You are angry."

Even if you know that you know that you are on His bad side, ask for His mercy even though He is angry. If He's done it before, He will do it again. Ask Him! Give Him praise of thanks even through the painful process. I understand that things can look too dark to find anything to be thankful for. Sometimes you have to just praise Him for what *didn't* happen. You may be frustrated and angry because you got a flat tire you can't afford to fix, but you can thank Him for the car accident that He may have kept you from being involved in down the road. You just never know why things happen the way they do when you're trusting in God.

How to Deal: *With the Present*

Colossians 4:2 "Be persistent in prayer, and keep alert as you pray, giving thanks to God."

A thankful heart is a vital part of prayer. Even when you are struggling, even when you've lost it all, give thanks to God for what you do have. If you're still alive, God still has a purpose for you. Don't give up, don't discount yourself. There is so much more to life than what you see right now; don't quit. Thank Him for what's coming. His promises are just as much yours as they are mine, be thankful for them!

Matthew 13:12 "For the person who has something will be given more, so that he will have more than enough; but the person who has nothing will have taken away from him even the little he has."

Have your parents ever told you, "Quit crying or I'll give you something to cry about"? That's what I think of when I read this scripture. If you spend all your energy crying and focusing about what didn't work out or what didn't go your way or what you didn't get, well you just may be given more to cry about. But if you are thankful for what you *do* have…He'll give us more to be thankful for.

Focus on the goodness of God. Even if the majority of life right now is negative or bad, focus on and appreciate the little joys in life. "For the person who has something will be given more" if you choose to have joy, you will be given more joy. If you choose to have misery and focus on the hurt and pain, you will be given more. Choose joy! Choose gratitude.

It makes sense if you think about it. Think about giving your child, parent, or friend a gift; if they express great gratitude for that gift, how much more do you want to bless them again in the future? As opposed to giving someone a gift and they toss it back in the bag and move on to the next one or just toss it aside and say, "I would have preferred cash." Well, you'll probably be less enthusiastic to gift them anything again the next time. So be thankful for every little thing. Be hopeful, and He will give you all the more hope.

Job 35:9-10 "When people are oppressed, they groan; they cry for someone to save them. But they don't turn to God, their Creator, who gives them hope in their darkest hours."

We always want to turn to another person for help and hope. We go to our friend, our pastor, our mother, our sister, our brother, aunty, granny, *social media*...the truth is, people may help Band-Aid the hurt, but only God, your Creator, can truly help, heal, and bring you hope in any situation. The unfortunate truth, however, is most of us will talk through it with every other option before *finally* taking it to God, as a last resort. Turn to God first, tell Him what you need, thank Him that you woke up today, you didn't have any choice in the matter, that was God's work. Thank Him that you escaped the work of the enemy today, that wasn't by your own strength or wisdom, that was God!

Zephaniah 1:12 "I will punish the people who are self-satisfied and confident, who say to themselves, 'The Lord never does anything, one way or the other.'"

He does so much more for us in the little things than we could ever recognize! Don't think you can manipulate God by saying, "Oh, God never moves in *my* life, poor me, He never does anything for *me*. I've had to do all this on my own." This will not get God's attention to move for you, in fact, He will punish you for it. God is good, and He is for *everyone!* God is in the details! There is always something to be thankful for! There is nothing we can do in our own strength; human help is worthless without a move of God.

Repentance is another important part of your prayer life. This is where you see the answer for, "Does God love even rapists?" Yes, He absolutely does, and when a believer, even a rapist, comes to have a relationship with God, there comes a point of growth within that relationship where repentance is expected. That goes for us all. You should love

Repent, Forgive, & Pray!

God so much that when you do these bad things, you *feel* bad about it, and you *want* to repent for it, turn your life around and *stop doing it.*

Repentance means you confess to God that you messed up, *and* you *stop* the behavior. God knows we sin; we will continue to sin, and Jesus' sacrifice has covered our sin, but we still must repent when we do. Repentance is not simply apologizing for sin and continuing to do it, but you must also correct your path and *forgive* those who have sinned against *you.*

The Lord's Prayer in Matthew 6:9-13 is an example of how the Lord wants you to pray. If you break it down, it covers all you really need in a prayer. It's quick, easy and to the point. You glorify the Father and honor His Holy Name, you ask that *His* will be done, knowing and trusting that it will always bring you good and the desires of your heart regardless of what the process looks like, because He already knows what you want. You ask that He provide your daily needs such as the food you need to survive, you repent or ask for His forgiveness as you forgive others who have done you wrong, and you ask that He keep you safe from evil. This really is the perfect prayer because sure, we all want to win the lottery, but if we all prayed to win and God answered every one of us, we'd all get about a dollar. That's not a wise prayer. Pray instead, for provision, and *He* will decide what form it will come.

Joel 2:12 "repent sincerely and return to Me with fasting and weeping and mourning. Let your broken heart show your sorrow. —He is always ready to forgive and not punish. Perhaps the Lord your God will change His mind and bless you with abundant crops."

Repent! We know God is a good God and He wants to forgive you, but you must show Him that you mean it! He says repent with fasting and weeping and mourning; be sincere! He's just waiting on you to move. So, move! Confess your sins and pray! Pray for wisdom and understanding going forward.

Repentance comes with correction. Correction should always follow sincere repentance. Correct your path. There are some things that can't come with you, some mindsets you'll have to leave behind, certain habits you'll have to let go of. Not everything, or everyone, can go where you're going. If people are hindering you from making these changes, you may have to let them go. Better to keep the Lord and lose a bad influence than keep a bad influence and lose the Lord.

Repent, Forgive, & Pray!

Micah 3:4 "The time is coming when you will cry out to the Lord, but He will not answer you. He will not listen to your prayers, for you have done evil."

Prayer without repentance and repentance without change falls short; He won't listen to you. Back in college I had a best friend that hooked up with my ex-boyfriend after I broke up with him. She apologized and I forgave her, but she did it again. Needless to say, her apologies didn't hold any weight with me after that. Now, God's got a bit more grace than me, He won't count you out after one mistake, big or small — we're all learning, but I think you get the point. Work toward *changing* the behavior! You've got to at least *try*. Communicate with Him, *pray!*

Isaiah 65:1-2 "The Lord said, 'I was ready to answer My people's prayers, but they did not pray. I was ready for them to find Me, but they did not even try. The nation did not pray to Me, even though I was always ready to answer, 'Here I am; I will help you.' I have always been ready to welcome My people, who stubbornly do what is wrong and go their own way."

Did y'all know this was God's mentality? What! We act like we have to do all this begging, pleading, and convincing to get God to answer our prayers, but in reality, it is His *desire* to do it. He *wants* to answer our prayers, He *wants*

173

to help us, He *wants* to save us! He's just waiting on *us* to ask Him!!

Matthew 7:7-8 "Ask, and you will receive; seek, and you will find; knock, and the door will be opened for you. For everyone who asks will receive, and anyone who seeks will find, and the door will be opened to those who knock."
1 John 3:22-23 "We receive from Him whatever we ask, because we obey His commands and do what pleases Him. What He commands is that we believe in His Son Jesus Christ and love one another, just as Christ commanded us."

"You *will* receive..." "We receive *whatever we ask...*" All because we ask! You guys, a lot of people see God as this big angry guy sitting up on a cloud with a fly swatter, just waiting for us to mess up so He can knock us down, but that's not true at all! You've just got to know and *believe* that! Don't just think it, ask it!

Mark 11:24-25 "When you pray and ask for something, believe that you have received it, and you will be given whatever you ask for. And when you stand and pray, forgive anything you may have against anyone, so that your Father in Heaven will forgive the wrongs you have done."

There's that forgiveness word again. This is what I probably struggle the most with, not because I don't want to forgive, I do. I just don't exactly know *how*. How do you forgive someone who has done you so wrong? How do you forgive someone you thought was your friend but completely betrayed you for their own gain? How do you forgive someone who tore your whole world apart? How do you forgive someone who used you and threw you away with no remorse? How do you forgive someone who has hurt you over and over and over?

Matthew 18:21-22 "Then Peter came to Jesus and asked, 'Lord, if my brother keeps on sinning against me, how many times do I have to forgive him? Seven times?' 'No, not seven times,' answered Jesus, 'but seven times seven.'"

We have to forgive, and forgive *often*; but *how* do you forgive?? Saying it is one thing, that's almost easy; but how do you get your heart to agree? The truth is, I don't know that answer for sure, but I know it can't be done without a work of God! So, I pray, and I speak it, even if I don't believe it. I speak it until I can say it without cringing anymore. I speak it until it doesn't feel so fake. I speak it until I start to believe it. I speak it until the pain in those words begins to fade. And finally, one day, I'll see that person and I won't walk the other direction. I'll hear their name and my stomach won't turn. Eventually, one day, I'll get the urge to pray for them. And I don't mean prayers to cast them off to a deserted island somewhere far, far away where the sand is incessantly blowing into their eyes, never to return again; I don't even mean prayers that they get in return what they've done to me, I mean prayers of love and blessings.

1 Peter 4:8 "Above everything, love one another earnestly, because love covers over many sins."
Matthew 5:44 "love your enemies and pray for those who persecute you."

"God, bless them in all they do, touch their minds, reveal Yourself to them in a new way and let them be forever changed by it." That kind of prayer – and it's *hard!* Trust me, I'm not telling you it's easy, but I know it's right. And I know I'll be better for it. I know that God will bless me for it, and I know that I'll be blessed just to walk in that freedom of forgiveness, because there absolutely is freedom in forgiveness.

Ecclesiastes 7:9 "Keep your temper under control; it is foolish to harbor a grudge."

Holding a grudge will not keep them up at night, it will only hurt you. It's better for you to love. It's better for you to forgive. You cannot control everyone else, you can't even control what happens to you; all you have control over is how you respond to it.

176

Repent, Forgive, & Pray!

Luke 6:27-36 "But I tell you who hear me: Love your enemies, do good to those who hate you, bless those who curse you, and pray for those who mistreat you. If anyone hits you on one cheek, let him hit the other one too; if someone takes your coat, let him have your shirt as well. Give to everyone who asks you for something, and when someone takes what is yours, do not ask for it back. Do for others just what you want them to do for you. If you love only people who love you, why should you receive a blessing? Even sinners love those who love them! And if you do good only to those who do good to you, why should you receive a blessing? Even sinners do that! And if you lend only to those from whom you hope to get it back, why should you receive a blessing? Even sinners lend to sinners, to get back the same amount! No! Love your enemies and do good to them; lend and expect nothing back. You will then have a great reward, and you will be children of the Most High God. For He is good to the ungrateful and the wicked. Be merciful just as your Father is merciful."

Now let's not get it twisted, this scripture does not encourage anyone to stay in an abusive situation. The point is, there is no need for retaliation or revenge; that's in God's hands. All you need to do is love one another – no matter what! That is the greatest commandment after loving God. Anyone can love when they receive love first or in return, but it takes real humility to love those who hate you and pray for those who have betrayed you.

177

How to Deal: *With the Present*

Job 42:10 "after Job had prayed for his three friends, the Lord made him prosperous again and gave him twice as much as he had before." James 5:16 "So then, confess your sins to one another and pray for one another, so that you will be healed."

There is healing when you pray for others. There is prosperity in your humility. Confess your sins, God's healing is in your confession. His mercy is found in your confession. What do you have to lose? God already knows what you've done. Be real with Him.

Proverbs 28:13 "You will never succeed in life if you try to hide your sins. Confess them and give them up; then God will show mercy to you."

He knows...it's not about revealing to Him something He doesn't already know, it's about humility; can you put your pride aside and muster up the words to admit that you were wrong? Can you confess that you messed up? Speaking it also gives you a sense of accountability. You know it's wrong, you've confessed it out loud, now will you do it again? You've got to turn away from those things that had you bound.

Job 36:8-11 "But if people are bound in chains, suffering for what they have done, God shows them their sins and their pride. He makes them

Repent, Forgive, & Pray!

listen to His warning to turn away from evil. If they obey God and serve Him, they live out their lives in peace and prosperity."

There is peace and blessings in turning away from your sins and serving God. There's prosperity and freedom in repenting for your sins and humbling yourself. Try it and watch as your same exact situation with your same exact circumstances suddenly shifts, because the truth is, it is God who gives, and it is God who withholds.

Haggai 2:15-17 "The Lord says, 'Can't you see what has happened to you? Before you started to rebuild the Temple, you would go to a pile of grain expecting to find twenty bushels, but there would be only ten. You would go to draw fifty gallons of wine from a vat, but find only twenty. I sent scorching winds and hail to ruin everything you tried to grow, but still you did not repent.'"

Think of yourself as the temple; before you started to rebuild yourself in Christ, everything fell short. Nothing you did was ever good enough. You always seemed to just get by. But now, by rebuilding yourself in Christ, by confessing your sins and giving them to God, by repenting for your past and turning away from your sins, God will restore you.

Zechariah 3:4 "I have taken away your sin and will give you new clothes to wear."

This scripture speaks about removing your sin and figuratively clothing you in the new, but it really spoke in a literal sense to my situation. After the series of unfortunate events we were in I had one outfit; a pair of leggings, a tank top, a cropped hoodie and one pair of shoes that I was wearing on my body that day. I couldn't afford to replace anything. I was so frustrated and embarrassed, and I couldn't afford to do anything about it. But when, in complete lack and devastation, I confessed and repented and prayed, God removed my sin and gave me new clothes to wear, spiritual clothes *and* physical clothes, since I had lost all of mine and couldn't afford to replace anything, and some of these new clothes I've found on a budget on sale racks are even better than the designer clothes I lost! It had been months of living in that one same outfit, but He responded when I made the first move, and He restored better than what I had lost, because He is a "better than" God.

Job 42:12 "The Lord blessed the last part of Job's life more than He blessed the first."

Better than, but the key is to repent! Ask God to forgive your sins and the sins of your ancestors. It may not have even been something you've done it may be generational. You may feel as though you've done nothing to deserve what you're going through, like Job.

Job 9:15 "Though I am innocent, all I can do is beg for mercy from God, my judge."

Don't sit and wallow in how unfair it seems; you've got to pray. Beg for mercy and repent for the sins of yourself *and* those of your ancestors as well. Break off any generational curses.

Zechariah 1:2 "I, the Lord, was very angry with your ancestors, but now I say to you, return to Me, and I will return to you."

All He asks is that you return to Him and confess your past. There's nothing too dark or too disgusting; He can handle it! The worse the scenario, the more grace God has.

Romans 5:20 "… but where sin is increased, God's grace is increased much more."

God has endless grace for all sin, but you must confess it! He will forgive you and do what is right, He promised! You can be made pure through your confession. He will wash your sins clean!

How to Deal: *With the Present*

1 John 1:9 "But if we confess our sins to God, He will keep His promise and do what is right: He will forgive us our sins and purify us from all our wrongdoing."

It's really that simple! There was a time, before Jesus came, that you would have to bring a sacrifice to God that was pleasing to Him to cover your sins; but Jesus came and became a sacrifice for all our sin. Now it is as easy as asking and receiving. All you have to do is open your mouth and ask! Jesus pleads to God on our behalf! He approaches the throne of God, without sin or fault, and pleads for our forgiveness!

1 John 2:1-2 "But if anyone does sin, we have someone who pleads with the Father on our behalf — Jesus Christ, the righteous one. And Christ Himself is the means by which our sins are forgiven, and not our sins only, but also the sins of everyone."

We are forgiven based upon our confession, repentance, and prayer, but also on the basis of how we ourselves, forgive others. This goes back to the Lord's Prayer, "forgive us our trespasses, as we forgive those who trespass against us." Forgive me, *as* I forgive them.

Matthew 6:14 "If you forgive others the wrongs they have done to you, your Father in Heaven will also forgive you."

Repent, Forgive, & Pray!

Again, *if* you forgive, *then* He will forgive. Of course, it's hard to forgive, but it's much harder to not receive the Father's forgiveness. I just want to show you all a few examples from the Bible of just how important and powerful the forgiveness of your sins actually is. In the book of Luke, the paralyzed man who was brought to Jesus was unable to get into the crowded house through the door, but they were determined, so they lowered him in through the roof…

Luke 5:20 "When Jesus saw how much faith they had, He said to the man, 'Your sins are forgiven, My friend.'"

Through his faith and the forgiveness of his sins he was healed to get up and walk. A lot of people leave this part out of their prayers. You've got to repent. Confess your sins to Him; be honest with Him about it. He wants to love us, He wants to forgive us, it is His desire to save us!

Micah 7:18-20 "There is no other god like You, O Lord; You forgive the sins of Your people who have survived. You do not stay angry forever, but You take pleasure in showing us Your constant love. You will be merciful to us once again. You will trample our sins underfoot and send them to the bottom of the sea! You will show Your faithfulness and constant love to Your people — as You promised our ancestors long ago."

How to Deal: *With the Present*

Now, as you're coming into prayer, it is vital to seek wisdom and revelation of His Word and His will. He will not withhold wisdom from you. Ask and believe that you have received it, not because you are wise, but because God has given you wisdom.

I put off writing this book for five whole years after I had started it, because I thought there was no way that I had the skills to take on such a process. I'm not a writer, I'm surely not an author or publisher, I haven't studied or worked in any area that would have prepared me for this. I wrote every word of this book, I haven't had a bit of help, but who would want to read what I have to say? But then I realized, it's not my wisdom that's leading this book, I am fully dependent on the wisdom of God to complete this book.

Proverbs 3:15-17 "Wisdom is more valuable than jewels; nothing you could want can compare with it. Wisdom offers you long life, as well as wealth and honor. Wisdom can make your life pleasant and lead you safely through it."
James 1:5-6 "But if any of you lack wisdom, you should pray to God, who will give it to you; because God gives generously and graciously to all. But when you pray, you must believe and not doubt at all."

I encourage you to study His Word, seek His will for your life and gain an understanding of what He has for you.

Repent, Forgive, & Pray!

What He wants for you will always be better than anything you could ask, because here's a little secret, *He knows more than you.* He knows it all! He knows the beginning and the end!

Proverbs 2:3-5 "Yes, beg for knowledge; plead for insight. Look for it as hard as you would for silver or some hidden treasure. If you do, you will know what it means to fear the Lord and you will succeed in learning about God."

God will not answer certain prayers that are outside of His will for you. He won't give you every relationship you think you want, fortunately for me! Because as much as you think you want it, He knows better! So, if you're not getting what you ask for in prayer, consider what it is you're asking. Maybe rather than praying for that specific man to be changed so he'll treat you better and you'll live happily ever after with him (I've tried those prayers), maybe pray instead for God to send you the man *He* has for you, the man that will treat you right from the start, a man who you can build a life with. Don't just get angry with God and give up on Him because He knows better than to give you what you asked for. Adjust your thinking. Adjust your prayers. "*Your* will be done."

James 4:2-3 "You want things, but you cannot have them, so you are ready to kill; you strongly desire things, but you cannot get them, so you

185

quarrel and fight. You do not have what you want because you do not ask God for it. And when you ask, you do not receive it, because your motives are bad; you ask for things to use for your own pleasures."

We see this all too often, and increasingly more; people wanting material things so badly they are willing to steal, fight, and even kill for them. It may even be that they act out of desperation to survive or feed their family, but this is not the only option for survival. If only we knew better, I believe we could all do better. Be constant in prayer, even if you're not seeing results. Do. Not. Quit! Put your faith in Him. Y'all, I get discouraged all the time! And I'll admit, I'm not perfect, there will be times I go weeks without praying because I had prayed for something and God didn't exactly answer it the way I had hoped and I begin to feel like He's not listening to me, but Jesus explained it best:

Luke 18:1-8 "Then Jesus told His disciples a parable to teach them that they should always pray and never become discouraged. 'In a certain town there was a judge that neither feared God nor respected people. And there was a widow in that same town who kept coming to him and pleading for her rights, saying, 'Help me against my opponent!' For a long time the judge refused to act, but at last he said to himself, 'Even though I don't fear God or respect people, yet because of all the trouble this widow is giving me, I will see to it that she gets her rights. If I don't, she will keep on coming and finally wear me out!' And the Lord continued, 'Listen to what that corrupt judge said. Now, will God not judge in favor of His own people who cry to Him day and night for help? Will He be slow to help them? I tell you, He will judge in their favor and do it quickly. But will the Son of Man find faith on earth when He comes?"

Call on Him for your needs, even if it seems you are being ignored and denied your rights as this widow did; don't give up and stop pleading with Him. If this judge who had no respect for people would eventually give in to this widow, surely our loving, merciful God will hear you and judge in your favor. So, trust that though it may not be exactly what you asked for, He will provide what you need and what He has for you is good. Don't run out on Him just because you don't *see* Him moving. Keep asking!

John 15:7 "If you remain in Me and My Words remain in you, then you will ask for anything you wish, and you shall have it."

This certainly doesn't mean that if you don't yet have relationship with God He won't hear your prayer, He absolutely will, but there is something special about the way He responds to those who hold Him and His Word in their heart. Those people have special access, they can ask for anything and they will receive it. And it goes without saying that they would ask according to His will because when you have relationship like that with the King of kings, you wouldn't likely desire to ask anything outside of His will. If you know God's Word, then you know His will, and if His Word remains in you and in your prayers, then you will receive what you ask for.

Seek Him, seek His will, know His Word and claim His promises. To seek Him isn't just reading a couple scriptures here and there, it isn't attending church regularly, it isn't listening to Christian music; you must seek Him personally with your whole heart. We know if there is something or someone we really like on earth we will invest the time and resources to seek more of it, to get closer to them, to know them more, to know everything about them. How much more, then, should we invest in seeking God, our Creator and provider.

Jeremiah 29:13 "You will seek Me and you will find Me because you will seek Me with all your heart."
Psalm 37:4 "Seek your happiness in the Lord, and He will give you your hearts desire."

God is not difficult to find, seek Him and you will find Him, seek Him with all your heart. Don't let the promises God has for you pass you by. He *promises* to give you your hearts desire. Cry out to Him and claim what belongs to you as a child of God! Claim your inheritance! His Word is His contract – it cannot be broken. God is not a man that He should lie. He will hear your cries and answer you.

Lamentations 3:55- "From the bottom of the pit, O Lord, I cried out to You, and when I begged You to listen to my cry, You heard. You answered me and told me not to be afraid. You came to my rescue, Lord, and saved my life. Judge in my favor; You know the wrongs done against me."

God knows everything you go through; He knows every time someone has done you wrong. The hard truth is, sometimes we must suffer in the process of getting to our blessing and ultimately our destiny; most, if not all of us do. But it is His will, and you can trust that His reward will be great at the end of it all if you just hold out and trust in Him.

Consider Jesus' suffering and crucifixion; He could have easily called upon God to make it all stop. The humanity in all of us wants the suffering to end, but God knew the eternal impact of Jesus' suffering, and Jesus was compliant with the Father's will, even to death.

Matthew 26:39 "My Father, if it is possible, take this cup of suffering from Me! Yet not what I want, but what You want."

How to Deal: *With the Present*

Matthew 26:42 "My Father, if this cup of suffering cannot be taken away unless I drink it, Your will be done."

Even more than Jesus desired for the pain, torment, and utter humiliation to end, He desired God's will above all else and had faith for the outcome.

Matthew 26:53-54 "Don't you know that I could call on My Father for help, and at once He would send Me more than twelve armies of angels? But in that case, how could the scriptures come true which say that this is what must happen?"

You can't always pray the suffering away. Sometimes it is essential in bringing about the perfect will of God; it is not for us to understand or comprehend, but simply trust that He is good, and His will is *always* good.

Now that your sins are forgiven, your conscience is clear and you've sought His will, go ahead and PRAY! If you haven't prayed much before, prayer can seem like a tedious, difficult, and intimidating thing if you let it. I can't tell you how many times I've just thought about praying or even "thought my prayers" and waited for God to move, but never actually opened my mouth and prayed! But the truth is, prayer doesn't have to be difficult!

Repent, Forgive, & Pray!

So, the first thing I want you to know about prayer is that you want to be sure that you're always praying in the Name of Jesus, because He is the only way to God. He goes into the presence of God without sin or fault and pleads on our behalf.

Hebrews 4:14-16 "For we have a great High Priest who has gone into the very presence of God – Jesus, the Son of God."
Hebrews 7:24-25 "But Jesus lives on forever, and His work as priest does not pass on to someone else. And so He is able, now and always, to save those who come to God through Him, because He lives forever to plead with God for them."

Now, first things first: KNOW WHAT YOU WANT! I cannot even believe the number of times I've asked people what they need, what they're asking God for, AND THEY HAVE TO THINK ABOUT IT! How can you expect God to move for you when you yourself don't even know for sure what you want? Be specific! Write it down! That's why the Bible says, "Write it down and make it plain." You wouldn't believe how many people aren't able to answer that simple question. That also shows me that they haven't been taking it to God in prayer; if they were, they would be speaking and hearing those needs repeated out loud daily and wouldn't have to think for a second.

How to Deal: *With the Present*

Habakuk 2:2 "Write the vision and make it plain."

Make a vision board to reflect daily on the desires of your heart. If you don't know what you want, how do you know what to ask? That's all you have to do, ask!

John 16:23 "the Father will give you <u>whatever you ask</u> of Him in My Name. Until now you have not asked anything in My Name; ask and you will receive, so that your happiness may be complete."
John 14:14 "If you <u>ask Me for anything</u> in My Name, I will do it."
John 15:16 "You did not choose Me; I chose you and appointed you to go and bear much fruit, the kind of fruit that endures. And so the Father will give you <u>whatever you ask</u> of Him in My Name."

Again, don't just think it, speak it! You have to open your mouth and pray to the Lord, don't just think your prayers, let them be heard! Could you imagine how awful it would be if God answered all your *thoughts?!*

Sometimes it's hard to find the words to say when you start your prayer. I mean, this is *God* you're talking to! But you don't have to break out a dictionary in order to get God's attention. The Bible says:

Repent, Forgive, & Pray!

Matthew 6:7 "When you pray, do not use a lot of meaningless words, as the pagans do, who think their gods will hear them because their prayers are long."

You don't have to try to impress Him with your complex words or long epic poems, and your prayers should never be intended to impress others. In fact, the Bible suggests that you go off to be alone when you pray.

Matthew 6:6 "But when you pray, go to your room, close the door and pray to your Father, who is unseen. And your Father who sees what you do in private, will reward you."
Acts 9:40 "Peter put them all out of the room, and knelt down and prayed."

Just be real with Him! Talk to Him like a friend, talk to Him as if you were talking to a physical person sitting before you who had the power to change all your circumstances. If such a man existed on earth and approached you of all people, and called you out of a crowd, and said, "I can give you whatever is it you want. What do you desire most? What can I do for you? Ask me and you will have it." Really, think about it! How desperately would you be asking for your body to be healed? How desperately would you be asking for your family to be saved? How desperately, on your knees, would you be asking for him to restore your possessions and increase your finances?! Y'all, I would be on my face sobbing the ugliest cries the world had ever seen, just desperate! That's how Jesus prayed, and that is exactly how I pray to God in my alone time.

Hebrews 5:7 "In His life on earth Jesus made His prayers and requests with loud cries and tears to God,"
Luke 22:44 "In great anguish He prayed even more fervently; His sweat was like drops of blood falling to the ground."

I'm not even kidding. Snot bubbles and all. Because although no such physical being exists here on earth, God is that real, and He has that power. So, get real! Get emotional! Get passionate. Claim what it is you want!

Matthew 11:12 "…until now the Kingdom of Heaven suffereth violence, and the violent take it by force." KJV
James 5:16 "The effectual fervent prayer of a righteous man availeth much." KJV

Now let me just say, I don't believe there is any right or wrong way to pray; I absolutely believe that God hears and answers *all* our prayers, however, I believe there is favor found in certain prayers when you know what and how to pray specifically, effectually, and fervently. Know what belongs to you; you endured sadness for a season, but now you know happiness is yours, take it!

Psalms 90:15 "Give us now as much happiness as the sadness You gave us during all our years of misery."

God is your protector, claim it! Don't just lie down and be defeated, God has promised to lead you and save you from the trap of the enemy. Receive it! Don't pity pat your prayers asking God, *Lord, if it is Your will, would You mind maybe saving me from the...*NO! You know His Word; you know His will. Claim it! Demand it!

Psalms 31:1-5,7-10 "I come to You, Lord, for protection; never let me be defeated. You are a righteous God; save me, I pray! Hear me! Save me now! Be my refuge to protect me; my defense to save me. You are my refuge and defense; guide me and lead me as You have promised. Keep me safe from the trap that has been set for me; shelter me from danger. I place myself in Your care. You will save me, Lord; You are a faithful God. I will be glad and rejoice because of Your constant love. You see my suffering; You know my trouble. You have not let my enemies capture me; You have given me freedom to go where I wish. Be merciful to me, Lord, for I am in trouble; my eyes are tired from so much crying; I am completely worn out. I am exhausted by sorrow, and weeping has shortened my life."

How to Deal: *With the Present*

Be real about how you're feeling. Do you feel like God has forgotten you? Tell Him! Do you feel as though your trouble will *never* end? Tell Him!

Psalms 13:1-6 "How much longer will You forget me, Lord? Forever? How much longer will You hide Yourself from me? How long must I endure trouble? How long will sorrow fill my heart day and night? How long will my enemies triumph over me? Look at me, O Lord my God, and answer me. Restore my strength; don't let me die. Don't let my enemies say, 'We have defeated him.' Don't let them gloat over my downfall. I rely on Your constant love; I will be glad, because You will rescue me. I will sing to You, O Lord, because You have been good to me."

He appreciates your honesty. Don't think that by saying what you think He wants to hear or what you think would be pleasing to Him that you're doing yourself – or Him – any favors, you're not.

Job 8:5-7 "But turn now and plead with Almighty God; if you are so honest and pure, then God will come and help you and restore your household as your reward. All the wealth you lost will be nothing compared with what God will give you then."

Pray big! Ask for what you could only dream of! And recognize God in it when it comes. Because although God uses people, it is all Him behind it. If He blesses you through someone else, thank them for being the obedient vessel, for sure, but how much more should you be thanking God for the blessing!? There is no end to His miracles. He wants to do it for you; He *will* do it for you! More than you lost! Double for your trouble!

Job 5:8- "If I were you, I would turn to God and present my case to Him. We cannot understand the great things He does, and to His miracles there is no end."

You might not understand God's goodness, you might not think that you deserve to be blessed by God because the things you've done may seem unforgivable, but not with God. God's blessings are not something He rations out sparingly to the holiest of holy and perfect Christians, no. He desires to bless us all; He desires to heal us all. So don't make excuses for why you'll never be worthy of the blessings of God. Some people think they're being humble by accepting their faults and accepting that they'll just never get blessed. That's not humility, my friend, that's stupidity. You can actually talk your way out of your own blessing.

John 5:6-7 "Jesus saw him there, and He knew that the man had been sick for such a long time; so He asked him, 'Do you want to get well?' The sick man answered, 'Sir, I don't have anyone here to put me in the pool when the water is stirred up; while I am trying to get in, somebody else gets there first.'"

Jesus then healed the man right where he was. Even in the midst of this man's boo-hoo mentality, the Lord, in His endless mercy, blessed him. Why do we try to talk ourselves out of our blessings? Making excuses for why we can never get healed. We need to stop that! Be real with Him! Tell Him what you want, not what's holding you back! Don't make excuses. Don't block your blessings. Shut. Your. Lips! With the excuses! You have God given authority to claim what belongs to you, use it!

Romans 8:11 "If the Spirit of God, who raised Jesus from death, lives in you, then He who raised Christ from death will also give life to your mortal bodies by the presence of His Spirit in you."

"*If*" the Holy Spirit is in you; that means it's a choice. You have to invite the Holy Spirit to abide in you. But how?

Acts 2:38 "Each one of you must turn away from your sins and be baptized in the Name of Jesus Christ, so that your sins will be forgiven; and you will receive God's gift, the Holy Spirit."

Turn away from your sins and be baptized. The Bible tells us to baptize with water and with fire. The water baptism is to cleanse you of your sins, to be made new. The baptism with fire is to be filled with the Holy Spirit.

What does it mean to be filled with the Holy Spirit? To be filled with the Holy Spirit is different than being baptized in the Holy Spirit. When you give your life to Christ and accept salvation, you are baptized in the Holy Spirit. Ephesians 1:14 says that those who believe in Jesus for the forgiveness of their sins are given God's Holy Spirit as a permanent deposit guaranteeing our inheritance. Being filled with the Holy Spirit, however, is a continual process as you live in obedience to Christ. The result of being filled with the Holy Spirit is the gift of speaking in tongues, power, wisdom, authority, and the ability to perform miracles. The more you spend in relationship with Him, the more you will see the evidence of His power at work in you.

Acts 1:8 "But when the Holy Spirit comes upon you, you will be filled with power, and you will be witnesses for Me — to the ends of the earth."
Mark 16:17 "Believers will be given the power to perform miracles"

The Holy Spirit is wisdom and gives us wisdom and direction to maneuver through life's ups and downs. He teaches us everything we need, so that we don't need to lean on man to gain understanding.

How to Deal: *With the Present*

1 John 2:27 "But as for you, Christ has poured out His Spirit on you. As long as His Spirit remains in you, you do not need anyone to teach you. For His Spirit teaches you about everything, and what He teaches is true, not false. Obey the Spirit's teaching, then, and remain in union with Christ."

John 14:26 "The Helper, the Holy Spirit, whom the Father will send in My Name, will teach you everything and make you remember all that I have told you."

This is where the Holy Spirit comes in to assist with that *forgiveness* we talked about. The Holy Spirit gives us strength, compassion, and love. He comforts us when we've been hurt, abused, mistreated, betrayed, and gives us strength to forgive. Nothing else in life will bring you the comfort you need in those times of deep sorrow and anguish. The Holy Spirit literally *is* The Comforter.

Philippians 2:1 "Your life in Christ makes you strong, and His love comforts you. You have fellowship with the Spirit, and you have kindness and compassion for one another."

1 John 5:3-4 "For our love for God means that we obey His commands. And His commands are not too hard for us, because every child of God is able to defeat the world. And we win the victory over the world by means of our faith."

Repent, Forgive, & Pray!

Our faith in God gives us the victory over the world. *We* have the authority to cast out devils. You don't have to let them stay! The Holy Spirit in you gives you the authority to speak to your problems, speak to your enemies, speak to devils, and be victorious over them with the authority in *your* voice through Christ.

Mark 1:27 "The people were all so amazed that they started saying to one another, 'What is this? Is it some kind of new teaching? This man has authority to give orders to the evil spirits, and they obey Him!'"

Give orders to that which concerns you, you have the authority! And they have to obey! This is not a matter of, will we, as humans, defeat the enemy; the enemy has already been defeated! By Christ on the cross! All you need to do is speak it out! Remind that little devil that he has no authority over you. Jesus has given us the authority to tread over them and not even be hurt. He has given us the power to overcome! Use it!

Luke 10:19 "Listen! I have given you authority, so that you can walk on snakes and scorpions and overcome all the power of the enemy, and nothing will hurt you."

And finally, the gift of tongues. I've got to be honest, y'all, this one was strange for me in the beginning of my

Christian journey. Let me tell you, my first church service, there was a woman sitting behind me, we were all the way in the back, and she was speaking in tongues through the whole service – and loud. I was so annoyed! So, the next week I sat somewhere far away from there, service starts and there she is, right in my ear again. I turned to my husband like, *wow, is that really necessary?* I'm not even kidding you guys, for weeks, everywhere I sat, there she was. And it was like God placed her there to get me to get over my judgment and misconception of what speaking in tongues is, and it is very odd if you don't understand what and why it is; but it's actually super cool!

Praying in tongues is a way to pray when you don't know what to ask or how to ask it. I always pray my thoughts and desires and end my prayer in a prayer in tongues, just to cover all my bases! That is also another way to be sure to pray according to the will of God, because it is actually the Holy Spirit praying through you.

Romans 8:26-27 "In the same way the Spirit also comes to help us, weak as we are. For we do not know how we ought to pray; the Spirit Himself pleads with God for us in groans that words cannot express. And God, who sees into our hearts, and knows what the thought of the Spirit is; because the Spirit pleads with God on behalf of His people and in accordance with His will."

Repent, Forgive, & Pray!

Okay, how cool is that!? Almost always, I don't know what to pray about. But even then, He gives us an answer! He has made a way for His Spirit to come in our weakness and pray *through* us according to *our* hearts desire and *His* will. It's literally, the perfect prayer! Praying in the Spirit will present God the desires of your heart that maybe you're too humble to ask for, that seem like too much to ask. Praying in the Spirit rebukes illness in your body that you don't even know is there yet. Praying in the Spirit reaches God through the Spirit who is faultless and without sin, unlike ourselves. Y'all, pray in the Spirit!!!

Jude 20-21 "But you, my friends, keep on building yourselves up on your most sacred faith pray in the power of the Holy Spirit, and keep yourselves in the love of God, as you wait for our Lord Jesus Christ in His mercy to give you eternal life."

Receiving the gift of tongues seems very intimidating, I know. But if you inform yourself, relax, and stop thinking it's weird, it actually comes fairly easily. Once you have received the Spirit, you don't have to wait to receive the gift of tongues from any man. You don't need a preacher to lay their hands on you to receive the gift of tongues, although sometimes it does happen that way, as it did for me. But some people don't receive it that way and become discouraged; just know that you can just as easily receive the gift of tongues alone in your room, on a train, in your car or at the mall, as you can at the church. Just meditate on Him, get to an intimate place with Him, forget everything else around you and relax; and ask Him to speak through you. Begin to worship Him, just keep repeating, "hallelujah, hallelujah, hallelujah…" until He begins to speak through you.

Okay, now that you've got your prayers down, don't be rude; it's your turn to listen! Don't lead one-way prayers, pray, and then listen! God speaks through many things; it could be through a sermon on tv, a family member, friend or even a stranger saying something that *confirms* what you have spoken to God about. It could be a thought or feeling that is beyond your knowledge or ability. Listen for Him.

Zechariah 7:11-13 "But My people stubbornly refused to listen. They closed their minds and made their hearts hard as rock. – Because they did not listen when I spoke, I did not answer when they prayed."

Oh snap! Y'all, God will speak to you, if you'll just listen. And when I say listen, I don't mean wait to hear a rumble from the clouds and the Heavens will open and a dove will descend onto a burning bush, and you will hear the thunderous audible voice of the actual Lord God Himself. A lot of people mistake hearing from God as "listening to their conscience". Well, that's the Holy Spirit, my friend! So, obey that little voice in your head, don't ignore that tugging in your stomach, and if you question if it's really God, just know, His Word will always be good, it's always love, and it is always kind.

Proverbs 28:14 "Always obey the Lord and you will be happy. If you are stubborn, you will be ruined."

Malachi 2:2 "You must honor Me by what you do. If you will not listen to what I say, then I will bring a curse on you. I will put a curse on the things you receive for your support. In fact, I have already put a curse on them, because you do not take My command seriously."

That's some serious business, y'all. So, listen, follow His instruction. The Holy Spirit will lead you and teach you all you need to know for whatever season He leads you through. He wouldn't lead you somewhere and not equip you with all you need to succeed.

Micah 4:2 "He will teach us what He wants us to do; we will walk in the paths He has chosen."

If you decide to take your own path, you walk alone; but if you'll allow Him to lead you, you can't lose!

How to Deal: *With the Present*

Now the last big thing I want to share with you about prayer is to have FAITH! You cannot worry about what you are about to face. When fear comes upon you, He wants you to pray. What are you fearful of? Can you control the outcome yourself? If not, you need to do all that you can do and then ask God, by faith, to step in to handle the rest. It does not matter what *you* may have done to get in that mess, it does not matter what you've done in the past, God accepts *you*! And He *will* answer your prayers, but you've got to open your mouth and *ask*! Otherwise, you'll just drive yourself sick with stress and anxiety.

Philippians 4:6-7 "Don't worry about anything, but in all your prayers ask God for what you need, always asking Him with a thankful heart. And God's peace, which is far beyond human understanding, will keep your hearts and minds safe in union with Christ Jesus."

God is not surprised by what you're going through. He's not up there worried, as if what happened to you was some unexpected event that He, the all-knowing God, was not anticipating, no!

Amos 3:6 "Does disaster strike a city unless the Lord sends it?"
Amos 4:6 "I was the one who brought famine to all your cities, yet you did not come back to Me. I kept it from raining when you needed it most."

You can't blame the devil for everything. But why would our loving God, full of endless mercy and grace, do this to us? Or some prefer, *allow* this to be done to us? Either way you slice it, God will do whatever it takes to correct our paths. He will keep us from getting what we need most in order for us to realize that we are worthless in our own strength, and turn back to Him, and when we finally humble ourselves to do so, He will answer.

Isaiah 30:19-21 "The Lord is compassionate, and when you cry to Him for help, He will answer you. The Lord will make you go through hard times, but He Himself will be there to teach you, and you will not have to search for Him any more. If you wander off the road to the right or the left, you will hear His voice behind you saying, 'Here is the road. Follow it.'"
Joel 2:32 "But all who ask the Lord for help will be saved."

For salvation from your troubles, you've got to go to the *source*. Know God's Word and His promises and boldly claim them for your life in all your prayers.

Nahum 1:7 "The Lord is good; He protects His people in times of trouble; He takes care of those who turn to Him."
1 John 5:14-15 "We have courage in God's presence, because we are sure that He hears us if we ask Him for anything that is according to

His will. He hears us whenever we ask Him; and since we know this is true, we know also that He gives us what we ask from Him."

Again, if you know His Word, you know His will. It is not His will for us to suffer, however it *is* His will for us to turn to Him, and if that's what it takes to correct your path, He'll do it.

Job 36:13&15 "Those who are godless keep on being angry, and even when punished they don't pray for help. But God teaches people through suffering and uses distress to open their eyes."

So, when you're going through a season you don't understand, don't curse God or give up because you assume He's given up on you. It's quite the opposite. He's calling you closer.

Hebrews 4:16 "Let us have confidence, then, and approach God's throne, where there is grace. There we will receive mercy and find grace to help us just when we need it."

Listen to His call. Draw nearer to Him and be thankful, by faith, even in the process. Because no matter what it looks like now, we know He is good, and we know His intentions for us are good. It's only a matter of time.

Repent, Forgive, & Pray!

Habakkuk 3:17-19 "Even though the fig trees have no fruit and no grapes grow on the vines, even though the olive crop fails and the fields produce no grain, even though the sheep all die and the cattle stalls are empty, I will still be joyful and glad, because the Lord God is my Savior. The Sovereign Lord gives me strength. He makes me sure-footed as a deer and keeps me safe on the mountains."
Acts 2:21 "And then, whoever calls out to the Lord will be saved."

Chapter 6

Be a Blessing

It's a common saying when a believer tries to bless someone and that person tries to humbly reject it, the giver will say, "Take it, you're not going to block *my* blessing!" That's not just because it is a blessing to be a blessing to someone else, it is. However, the Word says that when we get to Heaven, the Lord will ask each of us, "What have you done for the least of these?" Blessing someone the Lord has called you to bless gives you an answer to that question when that day comes. It is, or should be, the *desire* of every believer to bless others.

God's currency is faith. He uses us to bless one another. If we are not obedient when God speaks to us to bless someone else with what we have, then how can we expect the one God instructs to bless us, to obey? If we have faith to obey God's Word to bless others, we can have faith to believe that the one He speaks to will be obedient to be a blessing to us as well. Be obedient to Him in the area of money and generosity and He will bless you.

Many people get to this point in their journey and say, "Oh, here it is, the *money* thing again…" But this is a teaching that will absolutely change your life, don't you *dare* skip over it! Ignorance is not bliss here, my friend! It is infinitely important that you understand the significance as well as the different types of giving because there are blessings attached to them. There are four main ways God instructs us to give: your tithes, offerings, first fruits, and alms. Now when the pastor comes up and says they're going to receive the tithe and offering, that does not mean your tithe, AKA your offering, as I had thought; they are two different methods of giving with two different promises attached to them.

Your tithe is the first and most important form of giving. This is the only one that God *requires* us to give. It is bringing ten percent of all your income to the church. Ten percent - no more, no less. Any more than ten percent should be given as an offering. Your tithe is the base to your giving. It is your obedience to God in the area of your finances to show your gratitude for what He has already done and already provided for you. It is your way of showing Him that you can be trusted to return His portion of what He has given and wants to give you. It is acknowledging that He is the One who made a way for you to have it, so you have faith to return His portion back to Him.

Ok, honesty time; it took me a long time to even begin to wrap my mind around the concept of serving and giving back, but *tithing?* Forget it! Here I am, struggling to get by, having to narrow down the five items I need from the *Dollar Tree* (yes, the place where *everything* is a *dollar!*) to four items because I don't even have five bucks to spend. So, a four pack of toilet paper, two boxes of spaghetti noodles and a can of spaghetti sauce would have to hold us over for the week. True story. But now I go to church on Sunday, and they have the *audacity* to ask *me* for a tithe?! I'm thinking, *these pastors don't need my money, I need my money!* And I was right, they *didn't* need my money. Neither my church nor my pastors needed my tithe, our church is well taken care of, as are our pastors. It *was* me who needed my tithe – but I *needed* it to be a seed, planted in that good, fertile ground.

I'm sure you've probably heard it said before, but it is so true, I used to think I couldn't afford to tithe, but now that I've tested God in that area and I've seen the results, I know, I can't afford *not* to tithe. Give it a try, you won't want to turn back!

212

Be a Blessing

2 Corinthians 8:2-4 "They have been severely tested by the troubles they went through; but their joy was so great that they were extremely generous in their giving, even though they are very poor. I can assure you that they gave as much as they could, and even more than they could. Of their own free will they begged us and pleaded for the privilege of having a part in helping God's people."

Now what would cause a struggling poor person to *beg* to help God's people? They must have seen the blessings! Y'all want to see a complete turn around blessing? Try Him! And I mean really, fully, by faith; bring ten percent of *all* your earnings to your storehouse (church) and see if God won't bless you. But I mean the full ten percent. Don't short God and expect to see the blessing. If you short Him, you'll only short yourself because He will return to you as you have given to Him. He knows what He has given you, you can't fool Him. So, commit to giving every week, the full amount!

2 Corinthians 9:6-12 "Remember that the person who plants few seeds will have a small crop; the one who plants many seeds will have a large crop. You should each give, then, as you have decided, not with regret or out of a sense of duty; for God loves the one who gives gladly. And God is able to give you more than you need, so that you will always have all that you need for yourselves and more than enough for every good cause. As the scripture says, 'He gives generously to the needy; His kindness lasts forever.' And God, who supplies seed for the sower and bread to

*eat, will also supply you with all the seed you need and will make it grow
and produce a rich harvest from your generosity. He will always make
you rich enough to be generous at all times, so that many will thank God
for your gifts which they receive from us. For this service you perform not
only meets the needs of God's people, but also produces an outpouring of
gratitude to God."*

If you've proven to be good stewards and obedient to
His Word, He wants to bless you so that you will use it to
bless others and He will get the glory! But you've got to know
and obey the Word, not just the action.

Early on, I figured I'd pay my bills, buy our food for
the week, toilet paper, things like that, and I would give ten
percent of whatever was left. Y'all I was sealing two dollars
up in that envelope like it was my firstborn child. I told y'all, I
was grocery shopping at the Dollar Tree, so two dollars was a
matter of "eat" or "don't eat" for us; it was "wipe" or...well,
I always made sure to get the T.P. But, ugh, I would cringe
every time and I was so resentful that this was a part of the
service every week.

I put my money in that offering basket, but I never
saw the blessings I was promised. Why? Obviously because
this was just some false teaching that snuck its way up into
the Bible to dupe us all, right?

Be a Blessing

Wrong.

I was performing the act, but not being obedient to what the scripture actually said. Before you do anything else, when money comes in you take ten percent to give to God, not because He needs our money to buy Himself the new Jordan's, but for us to show that our faith is not in the money itself, but in Him and what He is able to do with it when we give it to *Him*.

Give it to God and see what He will do with it. Watch how a hundred dollars will stretch when it's blessed. Watch what those three dollars will get you when you give to God. Your *ten-percent-of-whatever's-left* "tithe" won't get you much, if anything. But your faithful, joyful giving of your full ten percent tithe will get you more than you could have even imagined. It will make you eager to give the next time, but you've got to go ahead and start in order to ever find out for yourself.

2 Corinthians 8-12 "If you are eager to give, God will accept your gift on the basis of what you have to give, not on what you don't have."

You might think that even your ten percent isn't enough to be pleasing to God, that's not true. It's equal sacrifice. I thank God that He didn't call us all to give one set

215

amount every week, because to the millionaires on Wall Street, one hundred dollars every week is chump change, but to the single mom bringing home two hundred dollar checks every week, that's everything! God is fair and just. Ten percent of our earnings is equal sacrifice for us all and He will reward us with more than enough. He will supply you with blessings in order to be a blessing. If you are willing and obedient with the little bit of money you have now, God will provide you with more to do more.

The first time I actually gave the full ten percent, okay, here's the story…my husband, kind as he is, agreed to help an elderly gentleman do some handiwork around his house and yard every Saturday (literally his only day off since we attend and then serve at our church on Sundays). This gentleman offered to pay him some set amount of money for his help and although he never did it for the money, that little bit did help us out and we were grateful.

Now this guy was a bit of a grumpy old man, very set in his ways and the type that's "always right". I sometimes questioned my husband why he continued to help such a person (y'all pray for me) but he actually quite enjoys that type of person the most, (I mean, look who he married, he worked his way through my frozen little heart). Anyway, one Saturday he finished up work and was on his way out, my husband reminded the man very lightheartedly that he had not yet paid him. The man flipped out and threw a fit. My husband assured him it was alright, and he left without pay.

That next day happened to be the day which I decided to give God a shot to prove His Word. I put that ten percent in there with a cynical heart just fully convinced that no great blessing would happen to me. I mean, those stories you hear about, those things never happen to me! Well, we left service and were on our way out to our car and saw a yellow note on the windshield.

Now surely, I am not surprised that I, of all people, get a parking ticket, at a church, in a parking lot, parked in a perfectly good spot. Great. Such is my life. We get up closer and it is a note from that grumpy old man. See, we were so poor we didn't even have a phone at this time, so because my husband is always talking about church and God, this man, who was not a Christian and did not attend church, searched our church address, came and drove all through the parking lot of a church which has more than a thousand members, found our car, only to leave a note apologizing (which is a miracle in itself) and asking him to come by for lunch after church to pick up the money he owed him.

What!? I was stressing so hard about how I was going to make things happen without that extra income and then putting out a tithe on top of that?! But God restored both back to me instantly and I was able to do everything I needed to do as well as seed to sow for the following week. And I didn't even starve. Not once.

2 Corinthians 9:10 "And God, who provides seed to the sower and bread to eat, will also supply you with all the seed you need and will make it grow and produce a rich harvest from your generosity."

He will see that He can trust you with the little you have and provide you with more. He accepts even the small amounts. It's not about the amount of money you have, He doesn't want to leave you broke, and He can't spend it anyway, it's about the heart behind your offering and the faith you show in Him and His abilities.

It's about the sacrifice you are willing to give to Him. It's about saying, "God, I really need this, but I trust you more." It took an enormous amount of trust for me as a newly poor, new believer to put my full tithe in that basket for the first time, but I knew that I had to prove my faith in God somehow. Ironically enough, He proved Himself to me at the same time.

Be a Blessing

Mark 12:41-44 "As Jesus sat near the Temple of treasury, He watched the people as they dropped in their money. Many rich men dropped in a lot of money; then a poor widow came along and dropped in two little copper coins, worth about a penny. He called His disciples together and said to them, 'I tell you that this poor widow put more in the offering box than all the others. For the others put in what they had to spare of their riches; but she, poor as she is, put in all she had — she gave all she had to live on.'"

See, it wasn't about the amount of money, but the amount of faith and the heart behind it that was pleasing to God. Y'all, please try this! It does me no good, other than to see other people come out of struggle and poverty. I won't receive any portion of your tithe, I don't have a church, I will not benefit in any way, I have absolutely nothing to gain. But I ask you to try it. Commit to give ten percent for a year, six months, heck, even one month, and see what happens. But don't think you can cheat God and expect to be blessed.

Malachi 3:8-12 "I ask you, is it right for a person to cheat God? Of course not, yet you are cheating Me. 'How?' you ask. In The matter of tithes and offerings. —Bring the <u>full</u> amount of tithes to the temple. — <u>Put Me to the test</u> and you will see that I will open the windows of Heaven and pour out on you <u>in abundance</u> all kinds of good things. I will not let insects destroy your crops, and your grapevines will be loaded with grapes.

How to Deal: *With the Present*

Then the people of all nations will call you happy, because your land will be a good place to live."

Tryyyy itttt! Guys! Tithing is not just to benefit your church or for your pastors; although you do have to keep in mind that this is how some of them are able to keep showing up week after week to bring you this word that's apparently good enough to keep you coming back to receive.

You can't do anything else for free, so why would you think you should take advantage of going to church for free? We surely wouldn't like it if they started charging admission at the door, and neither would God, because God doesn't want your money as an obligation. He doesn't want to take it from you, He wants you to make the decision from your own heart to trust Him and give.

And please, *please,* don't base your tithes on how well off you think your pastors appear to be or what kind of car they drive, and don't hate on their success. You wouldn't choose to pay a broke doctor in a run down dusty old office to operate on you because you think the rich one's only want to heal you for your money. You choose them because of their ability to heal you, and for their experience and the wisdom and knowledge they bring. And that's something they should absolutely be rewarded for! The same goes for

220

Be a Blessing

pastors. The future of your life and well-being is in their hands!

1 Corinthians 9:10-12 "Anyone who plows and anyone who reaps should do their work in the hope of getting a share of the crop. We have sown spiritual seed among you. Is it too much if we reap material benefits from you?"

Pastors plant in us a seed of faith from the Word of God; an eternally soul-saving Word. Is that not worth at *least* ten percent?! Ten percent for eternity is not a bad price. My husband, who was a businessman for eighteen years always says, "God is the best business partner you'll ever have, He let's you keep ninety percent, and He only asks for ten."

1 Corinthians 9:14 "In the same way, the Lord has ordered that those who preach the gospel should get their living from it."

Listen, if pastors didn't get paid, who would have the time?? Who would be out here week after week saving sons and daughters and setting captives free after working a day job? There's a huge misconception in the church that God wants us to be poor and struggling because that's "humility", so they look down on those, especially pastors, who are wealthy.

Nope.

Just because they preach the gospel doesn't make them desire a good living and nice things any less than you do. God wants us to be prosperous. He wants us to be taken care of for doing good for the Kingdom of Heaven. They are saving souls; there is no greater accomplishment! That should absolutely be rewarded! They are an example of God's goodness when you obediently serve Him.

Some people have this idea that whatever a pastor earns, simply because they are a pastor, should be handed out to those in the congregation who are struggling. Well, if that was the case every pastor would be broke. Nobody else who earns a living and loves God is expected to hand out their earnings to everybody. Now, what a pastor should do is what often times people get most upset about. A pastor should teach their congregation regularly on the system and importance of giving so they, too, can be prosperous.

I cannot even tell you how many times I hear people say, "Oh, I stopped going to that church because all the pastor ever talks about is money." Well, in order to take up the offering, of course! Better they talk and teach about it than just say "Give!" or worse, just allow people to miss out on a blessing they never knew about because their pastor was too afraid to offend someone by talking about money. And yes, occasionally it is important to have a whole sermon or even a series on tithes and offerings because there is so much confusion about it and yet so much freedom to be attained from it!

My church rarely, if ever, gives out benevolence offerings because our pastor teaches tithing so well and those who tithe have no need for financial assistance. It is not a pastor's duty to financially support their congregation. It is God alone who makes us wealthy if we are obedient to His Word. Pastors who are obedient to the Word of God are deserving of their pay and reward. The bottom line is it is none of our business how another man, pastor or otherwise, chooses to budget and spend his money, and regardless of their motives, this is a teaching that will allow God to bless you. In the end we all have to answer to God and Him alone for how we live our lives. It is God who makes us wealthy, and the better we serve Him, the more He wants to bless us.

Deuteronomy 8:17 "So then, you must never think that you have made yourselves wealthy by your own power or strength."

Pastors have decided to dedicate their lives to being put on constant judgment by everyone; judging every word they say and every move they make. They become a slave to people's standards.

1 Corinthians 9:19 "I am a free man, nobody's slave; but I make myself everybody's slave in order to win as many people as possible."

I don't believe any successful pastor ever got into ministry because they thought it would be an easy way to get rich. Understand that ministry is not easy. They are held to an impossible standard and their entire life's work is on the line any time they make a mistake. People think that just because pastors hear from God and lead a church that they're obviously a perfect human being.

Breaking news – there is no such thing.

You've got to understand that they are people too. You can't give up your faith when they fall or slip up or do something you don't necessarily agree with. Just because the pastor's wife wears a skirt less than two inches below the knee that you don't find "appropriate" in the presence of the Lord, doesn't mean you should quit the church. Just because the pastor makes a joke you don't find funny or talks about a Biblical sin that you yourself consider "outdated", doesn't mean your spiritual life is *over!*

Be a Blessing

You're not going to always agree with everything your pastor says, and they make mistakes too! If they're human, it's bound to happen – but you didn't come for them, you came for the message, and their message is not their own.

2 Peter 1:21 "For no prophetic message ever came just from the human will, but people were under the control of the Holy Spirit as they spoke the message that came from God."
Philippians 1:18 "It does not matter! I am happy about it – just so Christ is preached in every way possible, whether from wrong or right motives."

If the word they deliver is good and you are learning, growing, and reaching salvation from them, then some of those minor things, you're just going to have to look past. Now I'm not saying you should support a pastor who lives an absolute life of reckless sin and hurts others in the process and steals, schemes and sells prophetic words for three easy payments of $39.95, absolutely not. But show a level of respect to a good pastor as a human being. Though they share God's message, they are not God, and they will never be perfect.

Thessalonians 5:12-13 "We beg you, my friends, to pay proper respect to those who work among you, who guide and instruct you in the

225

Christian life. Treat them with the greatest respect and love because of the work they do. Be at peace among yourselves."

We are always so eager to catch people slipping up and cancel them on the spot, especially pastors; but if God has grace for them and for us, shouldn't we exhibit at least a bit of that ourselves? Pastors are held responsible to God for watching over our souls; shouldn't we, then, show a bit of mercy on them? So, your pastor walked past you and didn't give you a hug or a pat on the back, have some grace! It'll be alright!

Hebrews 13:17 "Obey your leaders and follow their orders. They watch over your souls without resting, since they must give to God an account of their service."

A pastor's mission is to teach you and help *you* to prosper through the knowledge of the Word and wisdom of the Holy Spirit, not to scam you and drain your pockets. When you do well, they do well with God.

Alright now, moving on! Now, your seed or your offering is what you give beyond your tithe. This is where the blessings of abundance are received. This is the quickest way to debt cancellation. Your seed is your increase. It is not an alternative to your tithe; it is an offering *beyond* your tithe.

Be a Blessing

God's Word is that in your offering is where He will bless you with 30x, 60x, 100x return on what you give.

Matthew 13:8 "Still other seed fell on good soil, where it produced a crop – a hundred, sixty or thirty times what was sown."
Genesis 26:12 "Now Isaac sowed in that land and reaped in the same year a hundredfold. And the Lord blessed him,"

This is where people come out of poverty. Your tithe will rebuke the devour off your life and your finances, but your offering will bring the increase and bless you abundantly. Now you can't expect to just sit back and await a drop shipment of cash to land in your lap. The Bible says God gives us the *power* to become rich.

Deuteronomy 8:18 "Remember that it is the Lord your God who gives you the power to become rich."

This means that He will equip us with the wisdom, creativity, opportunities and whatever we need to become wealthy, but we must also put ourselves in position to succeed. It is His offer to us; the only limitation we have in receiving this is our disobedience to His Word. The first time I gave an offering beyond my tithe my husband was actually able to bless me with a Gucci purse for my birthday with the money we had saved up and it was returned back to us so quickly it was like we never spent it. I have to be honest though, I still have a hard time giving this one regularly which is strange because God blesses me every time! But I guess that's faith; I'll get there!

Alright now, your First Fruits offering is the sacrificial gift that you bring to the church at the beginning of each year. This is the big daddy offering, which, strangely I have no problem giving. It's the one that you sow with expectancy, thanking God, by faith, for what He is about to do for you this year. I am always eager to give this one because He absolutely blows my mind every time! My pastor always says you can't out-give God, so I always make it a point to give BIG for this offering, and boy is he right!

Nehemiah 10:35&37 "We will take to the temple each year an offering of the first grain we harvest and of the first fruit that ripens on our trees." 37 "We will take to the priests in the Temple the dough made from the first grain harvested each year and our other offerings of wine, olive oil, and all kinds of fruit."
Deuteronomy 26:2-3 "each of you must place in a basket the first part of each crop that you harvest and you must take it with you to the one place of worship. Go to the priest in charge at that time and say to him, 'I now acknowledge to the Lord my God that I have entered the land that He promised our ancestors to give us.'"

228

Be a Blessing

Leviticus 23:10 "When you come into the land that the Lord is giving you and you harvest your grain, take the first sheaf to the priest." Ezekiel 44:30 "The priests are to have the best of all the first harvest and everything else that is offered to Me...and My blessing will rest on their homes."

He gave you the harvest this year, whatever you have to give, He first gave to you, now give back as a show of faith so He can continue to bless you. The Bible says to bring the "first grain", I typically give the amount of our first week's paycheck, some give the amount of their first hour, day, month or even year – whatever the Lord leads you to give. Now don't be foolish and put yourself out, but remember that the person who plants few seeds will have a small crop, the one who plants many seeds will have a large crop, and since we can't out-give God I want to give big and expect bigger!

Think about it this way, when you pay a contractor ahead of time, you're trusting that he will do what you asked and discussed with him, and he's not only going to want to do the work (so he doesn't have any legal issues) but he will have to, because that's what the word says in the contract you both signed, right? Well, maybe not I guess, because contractors are human, and I hear a lot of horror stories around here in Florida after hurricane season, hm. But the good news is, the contract you make with God was not made with another man. God is not a shady contractor; He cannot lie and will not go against His Word. His Word is His contract, and He will obey it according to how you do your part. Honor Him and He will honor His Word.

Proverbs 3:9-10 "Honor the Lord by making Him an offering from the best of all that your land produces. If you do, your barns will be filled with grain, and you will have too much wine to store it all."

Give Him your best and He will give you *too* much! Now why would He give us more than we could store? Not only does He desire to spoil us, He wants to give us more than enough or "too much" so that we are able to bless others with the overflow, thus showing the love of God to others through our generosity. That's His promise! It's His contract with *you* that if you will honor Him above what is required (your tithe), He will bless you with more than you need and more than enough for what you desire.

How awesome is it that you don't have to give everything to Him for it all to be blessed? Boy, wouldn't *that* take some faith?! All He asks for is a piece. A crumb, in fact! When you give a portion of something to God, the whole thing is blessed, and let me tell you from experience, a portion of blessed money stretches much farther and does so much more than one hundred percent of regular money.

Romans 11:16 "If the first piece of bread is given to God, then the whole loaf is His also; and if the roots of a tree are offered to God, the branches are His also."

The first time we gave to first fruits y'all it seriously stressed me out. It wasn't much but it was a huge sacrifice for us at that time. We decided to give double our tithe amount. You all, I lie to you not, it was either that week or the next my husband had negotiated a deal with his employer and after months of not giving him even a raise, his checks literally doubled to the point that our weekly tithe became the same amount we sacrificially gave as an offering that day. From that point on I was afraid *not* to put that tithe in that envelope because I was one thousand percent sure that it came from God, and I knew if I wasn't obedient with that blessing, He could just as easily take it away!

The second time first fruits came around I had just been in a car accident where the Mercedes E550 my husband bought me by the grace of God two months prior for my birthday had been rear-ended by an Audi SUV while I was stopped at a red light and my car was totaled.

How to Deal: *With the Present*

The guy who hit me had state minimum insurance, so it only covered up to ten thousand dollars in damages to my vehicle and none of my medical bills and they had the nerve to *offer* me a rental car only to later deduct the cost from my settlement offer because the guy didn't have rental coverage! And worse yet, regardless of their offer, I didn't even want the money; for one, ten thousand dollars wasn't enough to cover the cost of my car, and for two, I couldn't find a comparable vehicle to the one I had – I just wanted *my* car back!

Well, the insurance company, repair shop and my attorneys all assured me that that wasn't an option, so we had saved three thousand dollars that we had put away to pay for expenses and found a vehicle for just that amount. We drove an hour to look at the car and had made up our minds we would just have to spend the money, give our first fruits at another time, and use that money to get the car.

We took the car for a test drive, and it had a few issues which we had expected from a three-thousand-dollar car, but it was decent, and we drove all that way and we needed *something* to get us around. But it just wasn't sitting right with either one of us, so after further discussion we decided instead to remain obedient and put God first and trust that He would work it all out somehow.

232

Be a Blessing

In the meantime, I had two different attorneys who both ended up dropping my case because there was nothing they could recover. They told me the best I could get is what they had offered which was ten thousand dollars for the damages minus the cost of the rental car which was around four hundred dollars and the storage fees which had incurred over the three months it had been sitting there, totaling around one thousand two hundred dollars, as well as the tear down fee of around one hundred seventy-five dollars. And that's not even including the sixty-eight dollars that was charged to my card when I returned the rental vehicle because the insurance company called me around 2PM on CHRISTMAS EVE to tell me they would no longer be covering the rental now that my car is declared a total loss and I'd have to bring the car back. That. Day. Well clearly, it being Christmas Eve, I wasn't able to return it for another two days, which was, of course, at my expense.

At this point I'm furious with God like, how? I pay my tithes I do what You ask, I trusted You with this!! I really believed that You were going to bring me victory in this! What is this mess?? No Sir, I am not having it!!

I asked my attorney if that was even legally possible, and he said yes, unfortunately they can do that. Well once my second attorney dropped my case, I was left to take their measly offer and settle on my own. Now it's just me and God.

I call the insurance company to take the offer and settle the case and I ask her, "So what is the offer?" she says, "ten thousand dollars." I pause and wait for the deductions — nothing. "Cool," I said, "So what do I have to do?" she said she would fax the offer to my attorney, and I'd just go in, sign, and notarize it and the check would be on its way. Awesome.

I go in and the attorney has this big grin on his face. "First of all," he says, "how on earth did you get her to agree to the full ten thousand dollars?" Y'all, I prayed so hard before I called that lady! Then I asked him, "if this is signed and notarized, they can't go back on the offer, can they?" He said no. Cool. Signed, notarized, faxed and we're finished.

How about the next day I get a call from the insurance company saying she forgot to deduct those few things and they were going to have to send me a revised document to sign with the new numbers on it. WHAT?! Now, usually I tend to go with whatever is said just is what it is; I'm not bold by any means, I'm from the Midwest, northern Minnesota, where we apologize when *you* step on *our* toes. We're basically Canadians. So, I just take it for what it is and thank you for it, but by this time I have just had it.

I reach back out to the attorney and ask him if this is legal. He again says yes, unfortunately they can do this. I'm like, oh no. I'm not having this, God it's You on my side now. You and me, no attorneys to get the credit, and I'm counting on You! And I prayed. "Holy Spirit, give me the words and the wisdom to get the victory. I refuse to take this loss." I called back and told them I will not accept this new offer. They assured me they didn't have more than ten thousand dollars to spend so there was no other option. She told me she was able to get the twelve-hundred-dollar storage fees waived but they would still have to deduct the other fees. I wasn't having it.

I spoke to the manager, and he tried to tell me that the initial offer was not, in fact, a mistake, but the adjuster was trying to make it easier on me so I wouldn't have to settle the costs myself after the close of the case. I said, "that's funny, because when I spoke to her, she said, 'I'm so sorry.' and 'I made a mistake.' Sooo..?" I told him this was a breach of contract and quoted a part of the document to him (*what?*). He said he'd call me in the morning.

235

Meanwhile my husband is trying to hype me up over the course of the night telling me I need to call back first thing in the morning and tell him this and that and be stern and be bold. And little meek-ol' me tells my husband of great faith, "I don't have to be or say or do anything, God is going to handle it, watch." He said "Yeah, but.." "Nope." I said, "God's got it. Trust me."

YOU. GUYS. That next morning 8:30AM on the dot, he calls me, asks again if I would take the new offer. I said absolutely not. He said "okay, we're going to send you the check for ten thousand dollars." I was in shock. Speechless. Finally, I said, "Okay. Well…then…I will look forward to it and, ahh, thank you." Great, right? I'm praising the Lord, couldn't be happier.

Well then, I get a call from the repair shop asking who would be picking up my car because the storage fees were about to be reactivated and start racking up again. I called the insurance company to politely inform them to go ahead and pick it up before their fees increase. And *she* asked *me* if I wanted to take the car.

Wait, what? I said, "Well, I didn't realize that was an option?" I immediately regret the words that just left my mouth. She said she would call me back. I was like *dang it man!*

236

I just blew another blessing! She calls me back and says, "It's yours if you want it." Ummm, YEAH, I want it! This is literally all I've wanted, are you serious?!

So, I call the repair shop immediately to tell them I'm picking it up and clarify that there will be no fees to release the vehicle. She tells me that the twelve-hundred-dollar storage fees and one hundred seventy-five-dollar tear down fees have not been paid yet and would have to be paid in order for them to release the vehicle. Are you KIDDING ME?! No way, I'm on a roll now, me and the Lord.

So, I call the insurance company back, she makes a couple calls, calls me back and tells me the fees have been cleared and it's ready to be picked up, however I would have to pay the tear down fees. Cool, I don't mind one hundred seventy-five dollars to get my car back. Then she continues, "but if you send us the receipt, we will send you a check to reimburse you." Look. At. GOD! Again, I didn't even have to ask, I was willing to pay it and *she* OFFERED to pay *me*!!

You guys, this is why I'm so passionate about this topic, because God is so good! But you'll never know until you find out firsthand! Things like this do not just happen to me!! They don't! Ever. Let Him in on your money thing! You want to ask Him to change your financial situation, but you won't give Him access to it! Give Him a piece and He will bless the rest!

Alright, whew! Now, almsgiving. Almsgiving is giving to the poor or helping others in need, without expectancy. It is giving to those who likely cannot return the favor. It is an act of selfless love. In doing this, God is able to use us as a vessel, but not the source, through which He is able to bless His people. In the same way, when you are in need, God will use others to bless you even when you cannot repay them.

2 Corinthians 8:13-14 "I am not trying to relieve others by putting a burden on you; but since you have plenty at this time, it is only fair that you should help those who are in need. Then, when you are in need and they have plenty, they will help you. In this way both are treated equally."

My reason for loving a lifestyle of almsgiving might be a bit selfish or proud, but I always like to give to others any chance I get to be sure that I give before I ever have to receive. I have a hard time asking for help, but I know that if I have given to others abundantly first, I won't feel so icky if I ever need to receive help. The best part about it is God's promise in almsgiving, that whatever you give He will return to you dollar for dollar. Our generosity is God's currency in which He is able to bless His people. He will use us, but never make us pay the price for it. He will return to us whatever we give.

Proverbs 19:17 "When you give to the poor, it is like lending to the Lord, and the Lord will pay you back."

How incredible an opportunity to be able to lend *anything* to the actual Creator of all life and things?! Not to mention the promise of a return, and you know that when God pays you back it is no small thing. But beyond the reward, it is our duty, as Christians and as humans, to love one another and to help one another and to carry each other's burdens.

Galatians 6:2 "Help carry one another's burdens, and in this way you will obey the Law of Christ."

By caring for others and carrying one another's burdens we obey the law of Christ. I find it so frustrating and borderline humorous when "Christians" will judge others for all their "sinful" ways, yet they, themselves, are outside of the one true and actual Law of Christ – to love and care for others. That's all He calls us to do!

We should never be in the habit of seeing another person struggling while we are able to help and turning away from them. This is where the "Golden Rule" comes into play. God is a generous God, whenever we are in need, He is eager to provide. But we know that God is not a physical being, He works through people, He works through us. He needs a willing and obedient believer to be a vessel and say, "Use me, Lord!"

Sometimes as Christians, we desire to be used for the masses, while we reject the one in front of us; but there is no difference to God in helping one and helping one thousand. If He needs you to help many, great. But if He needs you to help just one, are you willing? Are you willing to be generous as your God is?

Matthew 5:42 "When someone asks you for something, give it to him; when someone wants to borrow something, lend it to him."
Proverbs 3:27-28 "Whenever you possibly can, do good to those who need it. Never tell your neighbors to wait until tomorrow if you can help them now."

How frustrated do we get when we feel we are waiting forever on God's timing? But again, He must work through us as a vessel. Could it be that we are the ones causing the delay? He says that He is willing to do for us as we are willing to do for others, yet we ask those in need to wait.

Be a Blessing

He wants to bless us! The question is, do we desire to bless one another *for* Him? He wouldn't tell us not to tell our neighbors to wait unless His desire was to bless us immediately as well! Are y'all seeing how this system works?! He needs people who are willing to listen to His voice, His nudge, that urge you feel and we sometimes disregard, telling us to bless someone. And He won't just use us up, He will find someone else who is obedient and has what you need to bless you in return! Don't wait; don't put it off. Don't say, next time. Do it now, while you are able.

2 Corinthians 1:4 "He helps us in all our troubles, so that we are able to help others who have all kinds of troubles, using the same help that we ourselves have received from God."

God has created the perfect system! If we would just be obedient and not so self-centered, we would have a well-oiled machine here! His design is flawless if we move accordingly! Not one of us as believers would be without!

1 John 3:17 "If we are rich and see others in need, yet close our hearts against them, how can we claim that we love God?"

To love God is to love others and care for each other as He would if He were here on earth in physical form. For as

241

much as we know and expect God to love and care for us, we should also love and care for one another. We are His hands and feet. We are given the opportunity to love others as Christ loves the church; but He will always give us the free will and choice. He didn't create us as robots, programmed to do whatever He commands; He wants to see our heart in our actions.

This offering, again, is not an obligation, but I say if you want an exceeding abundant blessing from God, then we need to exceed what is just expected and do what is appreciated; go the extra mile. Perhaps you have the financial resources to help the poor, but you yourself need a blessing that your money can't buy you; God will bless you wherever you may be lacking, whether it's your health, an opportunity, a rebellious child, to rebuke the enemy, victory in a court case, whatever it is God will send somebody who has the answer to what you need to bless you.

Psalm 41:1-3 "Happy are those who are concerned for the poor; the Lord will protect them when they are in trouble. The Lord will protect them and preserve their lives; He will make them happy in the land; He will not abandon them to the power of their enemies. The Lord will help them when they are sick and will restore them to health."

Be a Blessing

You might be like me and see people on the street corner holding up the signs asking for money and instinctively turn away, avoid eye contact and pray for a glare on your window so they don't see you. Don't. Be merciful to them.

Proverbs 28:27 "Give to the poor and you will never be in need. If you close your eyes to the poor, many people will curse you."

But still, we think, *Why would I give my money that I work for to someone who's probably just going to use it to feed their addiction? I'm no enabler! I don't work just so I can support their bad habits! Why should they get free money? Nobody ever hands me cash on the street.* The truth is, those are His people too, no matter what mistakes they've made or continue to make.

Jesus *died* for sinners; and their sins are no greater or less than yours or mine. He loves them just as much as He loves you and He wants to use you to care for them as well. It's not important what they do with the blessing once we leave; what's important is that they see the love of God through us because more than receiving money, they see the love and provision of God through us.

2 Corinthians 9:11-12 "He will always make you rich enough to be generous at all times, so that many will thank God for your gifts which they receive from us. For this service you perform not only meets the needs of God's people, but also produces an outpouring of gratitude to God."

Not only are alms an opportunity for God to bless people through you, but it is an opportunity for God to see your heart, and bless you for it, and for others to see God at work in the earth; and scripture says if you don't care for the poor, many people will curse you. Yikes.

Matthew 25:41-46 "Then He will say to those on His left, 'Away from Me, you that are under God's curse! Away to the eternal fire which has been prepared for the devil and his angels! I was hungry but you would not feed Me, thirsty but you would not give Me a drink; I was a stranger but you would not welcome Me in your homes, naked but you would not clothe Me; I was sick and in prison but you would not take care of Me.'"

Because God says that when you do this for the least of these – the poor, alcoholics, drug addicts, prostitutes, liars, prisoners, and panhandlers – you did it for Him.

Matthew 25:37-40 "When, Lord, did we ever see You hungry and feed You, or thirsty and give You a drink? When did we ever see You a stranger and welcome You in our homes, or naked and clothe You? When did we ever see You sick or in prison, and visit You?' The King

Be a Blessing

Maybe you just genuinely don't have the money to give, well alms aren't all about money; alms is generosity to those who need it – giving food is almsgiving. Maybe you cooked and have some leftovers to spare. I was in the Dollar Tree one time (where, if you recall, not long ago I used to do my grocery shopping) and this guy who appeared to be homeless got caught and chastised for trying to steal a loaf of bread, sandwich meat and cheese. He ended up putting away the loaf of bread and only purchasing the meat and cheese and left. I went up to the register and purchased that bread for him. By the time I had made it outside it was like he vanished. A huge empty wide open parking lot and he was nowhere to be found.

I drove around and around until I found him, just to give him this one-dollar loaf of bread. But because I had been in that same situation before, I knew that it was more than just a cheap loaf of bread. I knew how important it was for me to bless him with that. I knew the struggle and the shame to not have enough to get what you need, and I know how much it would have meant to me to have someone step in that way. My struggle has given me empathy and compassion

245

for those I see struggling, which is something I hope and pray and will fight to never lose.

Proverbs 22:9 "Be generous and share your food with the poor. You will be blessed for it."
Acts 20:35 "In all things I have shown you that by working hard in this way we must help the weak and remember the words of the Lord Jesus, how He Himself said, 'It is more blessed to give than to receive.'"

It is a blessing to give. Even when you yourself have little, alms require little to give; yet it gives so much joy to do so. There is so many ways to give alms, you can also give clothes and belongings. Maybe you can't go out and purchase exactly what they need, but you can share what you already have. You can donate some clothes you already have.

Luke 3:11 "[John] answered, 'Whoever has two shirts must give one to the man who has none, and whoever has food must share it.'"
Acts 2:44 "All the believers continued together in close fellowship and shared their belongings with one another."
Acts 4:32 "The group of believers was one in mind and heart. None of them said that any of their belongings were their own, but they all shared with one another everything they had."

They understood that God had provided them with all they had, and so He does for us, so it is only right that we share it with others when we can. God doesn't bless us with more than enough for us to store it all up and keep it to ourselves.

You can also give alms by offering up a place to stay, maybe you have an empty guest room for a friend in need or maybe you can even foster or adopt a child. I totally suggest you look into adopting a teen if you are able – they're awesome! And they're too often forgotten about.

Hebrews 13:2 "Remember to welcome strangers in your homes. There were some who did that and welcomed angels without knowing it."

As someone who has been displaced from their home suddenly and unexpectedly and been taken in and tossed out as a family from multiple homes because my husband's friends cared enough to take us in but their girlfriends "didn't know us", so we were forced to leave, I know how much of a blessing it is to receive this act of generosity as well as how absolutely devastating it is to be denied it. No matter how it ended I am eternally grateful to those who took us in and gave us shelter in our time of need because I don't know what we would have ever done without them. I believe even in the transitions, it was God moving us to the next step every time, out of "comfort" and closer to our purpose.

How to Deal: *With the Present*

The point is, there is always something we can offer, even a drink of water. My husband has always been a very generous man, and I was always cold and more reserved. There was one day we were driving down the highway out of town and we were on a budget, so we packed a poptart and a bottle of water from home for each of us. My husband and daughter had eaten theirs, and I was saving mine because I know I need to keep a snack available in the event I reach the level of "hangry" because it's just not cute.

So, we're pulling off on an exit and reach a stoplight. There is a man standing on the corner holding a sign asking for money. We sit for a moment and the man walks toward the car. I, as usual, look away and try to sink out of sight and avoid eye contact. My husband reaches for my poptart and asks if I'm going to eat it. Now, if you know me as my husband does, you'll know this is a very dangerous sacrifice on his part. We've still got a long day ahead of us and I haven't eaten.

Well, he insists on giving the man my poptart as well as his bottle of water. I was thinking, this man is asking for money, he's going to throw that stinking poptart back at you. But this man was so thankful and appreciative, and I had to really check myself at that moment. It took nothing to change that man's day, even a little bit. And it cost us virtually

Be a Blessing

nothing. Yes, we were struggling too, we were on a tight budget; but in reality, we were fully able to bless him with *something.*

Matthew 10:42 "You can be sure that whoever gives even a drink of cold water to one of the least of these My followers because he is My follower, will certainly receive a reward."

There is nothing too small to offer that will please God. Even an act of kindness is almsgiving! There is a woman at our church, a widow, known to the church as Mama. She used to own a shoe store that had since closed, and she was giving away a bunch of her shoes – most of them new. She knew my daughter wore the same size so she invited us over to her house so she could look through them.

By the time we made it over there her size was gone, so she gave her one hundred dollars so she could go out and buy herself a new pair. After appearing deep in thought for a bit, she handed my husband and I each one hundred dollars as well. We tried and tried to deny the offer but, if anyone knows anything about Mama, there is no telling her, "No." She gave us the old, "You're not going to block *my* blessing! Take it!" This was such a blessing to us, especially at that time. She had no idea the financial situation we were in, nor did she know the ways which we'd be able to bless her in return, but she heard from the Lord, and she was obedient.

Turns out, Mama was in remission from cancer so every six months I was able to drive her two hours to her follow up appointments and back, and to any appointments she had in between. That's how God works. Even though I wasn't able to pay her back financially, money isn't what she needed. She didn't know it at the time she blessed me, but I had the blessing that she needed. Since I am a stay-at-home mom, I had the freedom and ability to take her to all her appointments. Neither one of us knew what the other needed or what the other had, but God connected us to be a blessing to each other.

Proverbs 14:31 "if you oppress poor people, you insult the God who made them; but kindness shown to the poor is an act of worship."
Proverbs 14:21 "if you want to be happy, be kind to the poor; it is a sin to despise anyone."
Hebrews 13:16 "Do not forget to do good and to help one another, because these are the sacrifices that please God."

Anyone can afford to give alms; and sure, sometimes doing good and helping others can be a sacrifice, but it's all just a matter of your heart. He sees what you do, whether big or small, He sees how you care for those in need and how you put others first, and He will bless you for it.

Don't look down on those in need, don't judge them, because at one time you needed help too, and surely there will come a time when you need help again. So don't condemn people, because all your decisions have not always been right. It can be easy for us to think, well I never would have made *those* choices or put myself in *that* position – but I'm sure someone holier than you could say the same about you in some area of *your* life. But at the end of the day, God has called us to *love* – it's as simple as that. It's not for any of us to judge. Even Jesus wasn't sent to judge, but to serve and to save!

John 3:17 "For God did not send His Son into the world to be its judge, but to be its Savior."

Luke 6:37-38 "Do not judge others, and God will not judge you; do not condemn others, and God will not condemn you; forgive others, and God will forgive you. Give to others, and God will give to you. Indeed you will receive a full measure, a generous helping, poured into your hands – all that you can hold. The measure you use for others is the one that God will use for you."

Dollar for dollar, blessing for blessing. He sees what you do, and He will reward you. He wants us to be eager to help others so that He can bring about the things that we ourselves hope for.

Hebrews 6:10-12 "God is not unfair. He will not forget the work you did or the love you showed for Him in the help you gave and are still giving to other Christians. Our great desire is that each of you keep up your eagerness to the end, so that the things you hope for will come true. We do not want you to become lazy, but to be like those who believe and are patient, and so receive what God has promised."

Imagine for a second a world full of Christians who were all obedient in all four areas of giving, each receiving blessings from one another as well as their reward from God for their generosity. We wouldn't have to depend on the government to disperse our money but rather, the church we give to would give back to the community, we would give what we have to those in need, they would receive with gratitude and give what they have to offer, and the Lord would repay us all we've given and provide all we need as if we had never lost what we gave in the first place. If we make God our "Governor" by following His requests, He will guard and protect us!

Proverbs 2:7-8 "He provides help and protection for those who are righteous and honest. He protects those who treat others fairly, and guards those who are devoted to Him."

Be a Blessing

When you are truly devoted to God, being kind and helping others becomes a way of life. You don't do it looking to make a name for yourself or for any kind of acknowledgement other than knowing you have bettered a life and pleased God. So do it privately, not to glorify yourself with your acts. In fact, the Bible says if you do these things for recognition, He will not reward you for it at all!

Matthew 6:1 & 3-4 "Make certain you do not perform your religious duties in public so that people will see what you do. If you do these things publicly, you will not have any reward from your Father in Heaven. — But when you help a needy person, do it in such a way that even your closest friend will not know about it. Then it will be a private matter. And your Father, who sees what you do in private, will reward you." Luke 11:41 "But rather give alms of such things as you have; then indeed all things are clean to you." NKJV

Now although there are many great blessings God promises us in return, we should never do it solely to be blessed or only when we are in need. After your breakthrough, continue to do it, do it joyfully. There will come a time when God goes from being the God of "Won't He do it?" to the God of "He did it!" But even if you are blessed enough to reach a point in your life where you feel you have everything you want and need, never forget to do good and help others because in the end, it's never about us, it's never been about us. It's about pleasing the Lord, doing what we were created to do, and helping others.

The truth is, even if we come to a place where every need and every want has been delivered, we will always have need of God because we were created to be dependent on Him.

2 Corinthians 8:7-9 "You are so rich in all you have: in faith, speech, and knowledge, in your eagerness to help and in your love for us. And so we want you to be generous also in this service of love. I am not laying down any rules. But by showing how eager others are to help, I am trying to find out how real your own love is. You know the grace of our Lord Jesus Christ; rich as He was, He made Himself poor for your sake, in order to make you rich by means of His poverty."

Be generous in your service of love. Anywhere you go, look for an opportunity to bless somebody in some way. Give back in your time, serve others. Find a good church to get involved in and don't just attend, find a way to serve! For me, serving at my church is what gets me through the week; it brings me so much joy! It brings relationship with others in the church and lasting friendships that reach outside the walls of church.

Be a Blessing

Malachi 1:6 "They lived in harmony with Me; they not only did what was right themselves, but they also helped many others to stop doing evil."

Chapter 7

Be Careful What You Think and Speak

1 Peter 1:13 "So, then, have your minds ready for action. Keep alert and set your hope completely on the blessing which will be given you when Jesus Christ is revealed."

We must focus our thoughts on those things that allow us to serve God successfully, while eliminating any thoughts that would trip us up. We must exhibit confidence that God will accomplish all that He promised He would do. These things are strongly steered by both our thoughts and our words.

Be Careful What You Think and Speak

Unfortunately, many of us have been programmed to speak word curses over ourselves without even knowing it!

"My back is *killing* me!"

"I'm catching a cold."

"I'll *never* get that job."

"Looks like I'll *never* get married!"

"I'm coming down with the flu."

"*My* arthritis is acting up."

Proverbs 18:21 "What you say can preserve life or destroy it; so you must accept the consequences of your words."

Zaaaangg!! You've got to be extremely careful not to speak sickness, failure, and defeat over your life. **Be careful what you say!** You may very well have arthritis, but don't claim it as "*my* arthritis" you don't claim that mess! You can easily talk your way into or out of sickness or blessings. You think your words aren't powerful?

James 3:2 "All of us often make mistakes. But if a person never makes a mistake in what he says, he is perfect and is also able to control his whole being."

Perfect? Able to control your whole being!? Just by controlling your *words*? That is powerful, y'all! So much for sticks and stones…the words you speak determine where you go in life; they control your whole being!

Matthew 12:36-37 "You can be sure that on the Judgment Day you will have to give an account of every useless word you have ever spoken. Your words will be used to judge you — to declare you either innocent or guilty."

Never underestimate the power of your words. Every useless word ever spoken will be used to judge you. Don't respond out of anger and say hurtful things you will regret. You can be passionate about something without being profane. Everything that needs to be said, can be said in kindness.

Even your thoughts can determine your outcome; think positive! Your life is shaped by your thoughts. Think about it; you wouldn't just go to the grocery store without first *thinking* that you need food. You wouldn't just apply to a job without first *thinking* that you need money and that this certain place would be conducive to that process.

Proverbs 4:23 "Be careful how you think; your life is shaped by your thoughts. Never say anything that isn't true. Have nothing to do with lies and misleading words."

Be Careful What You Think and Speak

How can we be sure to never say anything that's untrue? Speak God's Word! It's true forever! God's Word is truth, and His Word is good. Learn it and speak it to your situation. Speak what you want as if it already was. The Bible is full of blessings promised to *you*; you just have to *know* them and *claim* them for yourself, *claim* them for your family, *claim* them for your situation, *claim* them for your future, *speak* them into existence. The Bible says that God's Word is true *forever*! Have faith inside your heart and in your mind that this is not only true; it's true for *you*!

John 10:35 "We know that what the scripture says is true forever."

That means that those blessings, and what God says about you, who you are, what you can do and what you can have, didn't just apply to people thousands of years ago, they still apply to this day! God has already spoken them, so they *have* to be done! *You* just have to believe it! Speak it! Claim it! *That* is truth! Speaking doubt, lack, sickness, profanities, curses, and death is speaking lies and misleading words. *God's* Word is life, God's Word is truth. Speak *truth*. Hurtful words and profanities make you unclean in God's eyes.

Matthew 15: 11 &17-18 "It is not what goes into your mouth that makes you ritually unclean; rather, what comes out of it makes you unclean. – Don't you understand? Anything that goes into your mouth goes into your stomach and then out of your body. But the things that come out of the mouth come from the heart, and these are the things that make you ritually unclean."

People are so concerned about the calories they eat or the gluten-free, vegan, ovo-vegetarian, lacto-vegetarian, lacto-ovo vegetarians, can't eat pork, no caffeine…but will speak all kinds of hate and judgment out of their mouths. A healthy diet is important, but a clean mouth can change your life.

James 3:9-10 "We use [our tongues] to give thanks to our Lord and Father and also to curse other people, who are created in the likeness of God. Words of thanksgiving and cursing pour out from the same mouth. My friends, this should not happen!"

How you gonna praise the Lord in church on Sunday and cuss your children out twenty minutes later in the parking lot? I mean, I get it! Even the holiest of us want to drop a word or two on our children now and then; it's not about not having the desire to do so, it's about taking control of it when it comes upon you.

When your coworker says something that you regard as stupid, don't react with anger, hostility, and hurtful words; have mercy for them as the Lord has for you, you're not perfect. Every rude, cruel word will come back around and

Be Careful What You Think and Speak

affect you in one way or another, whether you notice it or not. Only a fool will pop off with disrespectful words and arguments.

Proverbs 11:17 "You do yourself a favor when you are kind. If you are cruel, you only hurt yourself."

It takes maturity to keep quiet and let success be your revenge. When someone provokes you and you don't respond with ignorance and arguments, they lose. They want to get a rise out of you and when you let them, they win by default. It doesn't matter how it ends, you've shown them that you care enough to get upset and therefore they win. You don't have to tear them down, believe me, God will beat them down far better than you ever could.

Proverbs 19:1 "Better is the poor who walks in his integrity that one who is perverse in his lips, and is a fool."
Proverbs 11:12 "It is foolish to speak scornfully of others. If you are smart, you will keep quiet."

In this age of social media bullies, this is such an important scripture. It *is* foolish to speak scornfully of others. It truly serves no purpose. Not for you, and certainly not for them. We've got to the point now where it's as if we forget that the people behind these social media profiles are, in fact, people. How foolish to think that bringing someone else down with your words or pointing out someone else's flaws will somehow make you superior or feel better about yourself? And I'm not just talking about constructive criticism or disagreeing with someone else's point of view for the purpose of providing correction or a new perspective which is also foolish most of the time, but commenting on someone's face – guys, you can't change a face, not really. People are born with what they get, there is nothing constructive or helpful about that. It's just cruel and nasty.

Proverbs 24:9 "People hate a person who has nothing but scorn for others."

I think we all know someone who is just a hater by nature. They're always finding something negative about everyone they see and feel it necessary to speak on it. They may say it to get attention, to make themselves look better, feel better or to make friends; they may even say that they were only joking, but jokes are no excuse to say hurtful things.

Proverbs 26:18-19 "Someone who tricks someone else and then claims that he was only joking is like a crazy person playing with a deadly weapon."

Be Careful What You Think and Speak

Words hurt, regardless of your intentions. Check your heart, control your mind and filter your words. Take captive your negative thoughts and fill your mind with the love of Christ. If someone is speaking negativity towards you, *you* have the authority to come against it.

If someone came to me and said, "I don't like your stupid blonde hair." I have the confidence to know my hair is dark brown and therefore their criticism holds no weight. It should be the same with our character. Someone can call me a liar and a cheater and a bad person, but I have the confidence in who I am to not let it affect me, because I know I am a good and honest person. Remember, other people's opinions of you are none of your business. You don't have to receive it. If you know your identity in Christ, you have the authority to tear those words down which are raised against the knowledge of God and *make* those thoughts obey Christ.

2 Corinthians 10:5 "We pull down every proud obstacle that is raised against the knowledge of God; we take every thought captive and make it obey Christ."

He says you are loved (John 3:16), His (John 3:1), worthy (Zephaniah 3:17), purposed (Jeremiah 29:11), accepted (Romans 15:7), set free (Galatians 5:1), justified and redeemed (Romans 3:24), set free (Romans 8:2), etc, etc, etc. Familiarize yourself with your *true* self, the way God sees you. Begin to see yourself through the truth from God's eyes; control your thoughts, don't ever allow the hurtful words of others distort that truth. Anyone who comes against these truths is a liar. And, of course, think before *you* speak.

Proverbs 29:20 "There is more hope for a stupid fool than for someone who speaks without thinking."

You know the saying, "nobody knows how stupid you are until you open your mouth and show them", well it's so true! Don't be quick to respond to someone's hurtful words with an emotional outburst. Often, silence is the best response, especially when someone is attacking you with negativity. Responding to negativity with negativity will only increase negativity. An argument only works with more than one party. If you refuse to engage, the argument has nowhere to go.

You decide whether you give power to other people's words. Think about it like this, if someone came against you speaking a language you don't understand, they could be saying the meanest, nastiest things, but it would have absolutely no effect on you, because you don't internalize it as

Be Careful What You Think and Speak

good or bad. You have the choice to internalize, the same way, words you do comprehend. Don't *allow* their words to cause you to become angry. *You* are in control of what you receive and how you receive it. I reject hurtful and hateful words and accusations. I receive the love and grace of God and His righteous purpose.

James 1:19-20 "Remember this, my dear friends! Everyone must be quick to listen, but slow to speak and slow to become angry. Human anger does not achieve God's righteous purpose."

Speaking hurtful words and profanities out of anger is ignorance. It shows that you lack the intellectual intelligence and verbal diversity to effectively dispute and communicate your feelings. Responding out of emotion rarely brings about the outcome we seek. It is better to step away and gather yourself before responding from a place of heightened and irrational emotion.

Keep your mind set on things above; keep a level head. Remember that God has a righteous purpose for every one of us. We may never know or understand the thoughts of God or the plans He has for us, but we cannot allow our frustration in the process to make us angry and block His righteous purpose. His thoughts are always good, and His plans for us are the same.

How to Deal: *With the Present*

Isaiah 55:8 "'My thoughts,' says the Lord, 'are not like yours, and My ways are different from yours.'"

No matter what anyone else does to get in the way or try to derail you from your purpose and destiny, nobody can stop or block what God has for you, so don't get worked up over the small stuff. We'll get exactly where we need to go. To assume that we know the direction our lives are headed is ignorant. Only He knows, and He surely knows how to get us there. Believe it. That's faith! It's not easy to sit back and let people mess with you when it looks like they're throwing you off your path, but God works in that. That is where faith is heightened. You don't really know that you're walking by faith and not by sight, until you are trusting Him to move you where you literally cannot see, plan or prepare for the step ahead of you.

The enemy wants you to lash out, draw back or change your mind. Like Job, the enemy wants you to just "curse God and die." This is the moment you need to increase your faith and be strong and very courageous. Trust what you know about God, more than what you don't know about the future. Without faith, it's impossible to please God. With faith, all things are possible in Him. Remember, the righteous will live by faith. He can use what appears to be destruction to shift you where He needs you to go, so don't fight it, let Him move you.

Jeremiah 29:11 "I alone know the plans I have for you, plans to bring you prosperity and not disaster, plans to bring about the future you hope for."

Don't get angry or upset with what you see, God has plans. Change your thoughts. Set your mind on Him, not on your circumstances, because He thinks in ways unlike our own. When we think anger, doubt, frustration, and revenge, He thinks joy, faith, peace, and justice. When we set our mind on Him, we can achieve those things! Don't waste your time on negative hurtful thoughts.

Colossians 3:2 "Set your mind on things above, not on earthly things.

Set your mind on Him, even above what you see, because only He can change it all in a moment. The God who formed the entire earth and everything in it in just seven days is the same God that can completely shift your situation in an instant! He has many, many plans for us; so, don't get discouraged by what you see now. There's another plan right around the corner and every plan is victory; even when it looks like defeat, He has yet another plan.

How to Deal: *With the Present*

Psalms 40:5 "...You have made many wonderful plans for us. I could never speak of them all — their number is so great!"

And finally, we can't speak about controlling the tongue without mentioning the nagging wife. Ladies don't nag your husbands. You nag them because they leave the toilet seat up, so they leave it down and you nag because they pee on the seat. You nag that they don't help you with the dishes, so they do the dishes, and you nag because there's food left on the plates. You nag about this, and you nag about that but meanwhile, nothing they ever do is to your satisfaction. Y'all, that's exhausting!

Proverbs 25:24 "Better to live on the roof than share the house with a nagging wife."

I've seen some of you women speak to your husbands and I want to climb up on the roof myself! That is no way to live. Nobody wants to come home to that! Would you? They say the wife is the thermostat of the home. Ladies, can we just turn down the heat a little?

Chapter 8

Be Patient & Trust in God

CAN I JUST TELL YOU...my husband tells me just about *daily* that I need to have patience. Well guess what, I have none. Probably the single hardest part of the process of life is this right here, to be patient and trust in God's plan and process. It is for me anyway.

We know that even as children, we find it hard to trust our parents. Especially as teenagers, we think that despite their age and experience, we know better. We tend to think we're always right; that is, until we become parents ourselves. Typically, it isn't until the roles are reversed that we see the errors in our thinking. We find that cake for dinner is not, in fact, the best life choice. We discover that the types of people we hang out with do significantly influence our lives. We see that premarital sex can be not only damaging but life-altering. That "experimenting" with drugs, even one time, can leave you dependent for life. Chances are, our parents did, in fact, know a little something about life. How much more, then, does God know about our life, path, and future?

Malachi 3:16-17 "In His presence, there was written down in a book a record of those who feared the Lord and respected Him. On the day when I act, they will be My very own. I will be merciful to them as parents are merciful to the children who serve them."

"On the day when I act..." This implies that there will be times when God will sit back and watch. Let me be even more direct, there will be times when God will sit back and do seemingly nothing! You may be facing trials now, and just because you may not see God acting and moving in your situation, doesn't mean that in time, He won't swoop in at exactly the right moment and change everything in a second; and it doesn't mean He's not moving behind the scenes and setting you up for victory right now.

For the longest time I was being told that God was going to restore what was lost, that He would put us back living on the beach, that it would be a place I would love, and it was coming soon...all these great things. At first it was nice to hear, it made me hopeful. I would close my eyes at night and pretend I could hear the ocean waves crashing outside my window, transporting myself to that place. I would even have these recurring dreams that I was in my home and right outside of every window all I could see was ocean water. Now, I had lived on the beach before, so I knew what it looked like to live on the beach, but this was different. I thought, *what in the world could this mean?* It was like I was living *in* the ocean or like, right over it. It was wild, but in my mind, not realistic.

Over the years we continue getting these prophetic words of wealth and success and restoration and eventually, after years of hearing all these great things, yet at the time being in a one-bedroom apartment and staring at the same tiny wall's day after day, I started getting angry. I was so frustrated with hearing what God was *going* to do and what He *wanted* to do yet seeing nothing change year after year.

My husband encouraged me to remain faithful and trust that God would do what He said He would do. Meanwhile, the prophetic words kept pouring in that the Lord was going to bless us to get us out of our struggle season in His time and it won't be in our own strength or because of anything we do or anything we work for, it won't even be as a result of our own relationships so that we'll know without a doubt that it's God.

Well, as someone who was never *given* anything and who has a hard time receiving even if it was offered, I'm thinking, *There's no way in the actual world. That's a nice thought but it's surely not meant for me.* I completely wrote it off. I drove myself crazy for years trying to figure out how I could make something happen, and guess what? Nothing! I got nowhere!!

People continually told us to rest in the Lord, that His blessing is in our rest, but that made NO LOGICAL SENSE TO ME!! So, I pushed my husband harder to work longer hours and more days and no vacations…for FIVE YEARS STRAIGHT! Tell me why after five years, some friends of ours invited us to stay in a beach house a friend of theirs rented for the week. While we were staying there my husband still continued to work long days and not take any time off. One of the days I had an appointment and we shared a car so he asked if he should take the car and just get off early to pick me up and I said no, stay at work, I'll drop you off and take the car, you stay and get the hours and I'll pick you up after my appointment. I could see the instant disappointment on his face; he was so drained and fed up. He was trying to be strong for so long working this job day in and day out and putting on a strong front for us.

We both realized that we had been preaching to some friends of ours about the importance of resting in the Lord and stepping down so God can step up. At that moment we both agreed that he should take the rest of the day off. By that point we had already been blessed more than I could have ever expected by a woman who didn't even know us, had never met us, but rented this beautiful, huge vacation home and invited us to come stay, I was in total awe; but I *never* could have expected the blessing that I believe was released as a direct result of that decision we had made to rest and put our trust in the Lord.

As a direct result of us resting in the Lord, we received funding for our businesses that following month which allowed us to move back to the beach to a condo, so high up that no matter which window you look out of, all you see is ocean water, *just like I kept seeing in my recurring dream!!* Every night I hear the waves crashing into the shore outside my bedroom window, just as I had imagined in bed back in our one-bedroom apartment. We couldn't afford it. We didn't ask for it. We *never* could have made it happen! But God had it all lined up. All we had to do was obey in the simple things.

When I tell you I could have never imagined a blessing like this! But I thank God for His Word, both in scripture and through the prophets, that encouraged me to make it through and not give up. To be patient and know that God has got it all in control. I had been on the verge of giving up so many times; on my marriage, on life. I wanted to run away and start over, at the same time I wanted to end it all. But glory be to God for giving me the courage to push through.

I had a student recently ask me, what use is the Bible when she's been through so much pain? How is this book supposed to fix anything, unless she just throws it at her abuser? Well, this is it right here. It is to encourage us when we begin to feel alone in our pain. When we begin to think that we are alone, and our circumstances are brand new. When there appears to be no end in sight.

Just because we have a relationship with God doesn't mean bad things won't happen; Satan is still the god of this world – the prince of the power of the air. God has given us all free will and choice, and the unfortunate truth is, although some of us strive to do good, some will still choose to do evil, but we all are given the opportunity to choose. Unfortunately, some of the good ones end up being casualties in the process. The good news is, He's seen this all before and if you turn to

Him, He will provide you with the strength to endure and a way out.

Romans 15:4 "Everything written in the Scriptures was written to teach us, in order that we might have hope through the patience and encouragement which the Scriptures give us."

The greatness of the Bible is that we are given examples of people in the past who have experienced sin and salvation, loss and restoration, sickness and recovery, abuse and healing...these stories give us hope that the same God who did it for them can and will do it for us.

Our greatest downfall in trials is when we lose hope. The Bible is meant to give us the hope that we need to endure as we take our part in suffering. It is hope, along with our faith in God, which will be the anchor to our lives. God doesn't lay out the plans of our lives for us on purpose. But He does give us glimpses of our destination. We can choose to believe and trust, or not. We won't always understand what God is doing, why He is doing it, or where He is leading us, but these are the very things God uses to strengthen faith and build character.

Hebrews 6:18-19 "There are these two things, then, that cannot change and about which God cannot lie. So we who have found safety with Him are greatly encouraged to hold firmly to the hope placed before us. We have this hope as an anchor for our lives. It is safe and sure..."

There will be times you seem to be doing everything right and everything still seems to be going wrong. I've questioned my obedience, my actions, my prayers, my words, my faith, and my relationship with God; and I have come to this conclusion, it's not about what I do or don't do, its not about how often I do or don't do it, it's not even a matter of faith; sometimes it's just not the right time. Sometimes it's simply because we are still in the testing, still building character, still in preparation for what is to come, still trusting our Father who has the experience and knowledge to know what is best for us.

Job 9:20 "I am innocent and faithful, but my words sound guilty, and everything I say seems to condemn me."

Trust in God, even if you know you're doing right by Him and things are still going all wrong, sometimes He has to test you, to bless you. And I truly believe the bigger the test, the greater He'll bless.

I had someone else ask me recently about a man who lost his wife. He refused to listen to their Godly comfort because, "How could a good God allow this to happen?" My response, look at Job. God repeatedly blesses those who have been through persecution, so long as they remain in Him.

James 1:12 "Blessed is the man who remains steadfast under trial, for when he has stood the test he will receive the crown of life, which God has promised to those who love Him."

Each time you get your inheritance He gives you instructions on how to receive it. So, trust in Him, even if it seems crazy! His requirements are not difficult! He might tell you to walk around a puddle 7 times – that's all it might take! Then He'll bless you. But will you do it, or will you write it off as a crazy thought? It's not that He wants to make it difficult to receive, He just wants to know that you hear Him and you'll trust and obey Him, no matter what logic says.

2 Corinthians 4:16-18 "So we do not lose heart. Though our outer self is wasting away, our inner self is being renewed day by day. For this light momentary affliction is preparing for us an eternal weight of glory beyond all comparison, as we look not to the things that are seen but to the things that are unseen. For the things that are seen are transient, but the things that are unseen are eternal."

"Though our outer self is wasting away, our inner self is being renewed day by day." As you see things falling apart in the natural sense, it is doing a work *in* you for your benefit.

How to Deal: *With the Present*

You are growing and maturing, and it is preparing you for an eternal weight of glory!

Humble yourself and rest in Him. Humility is key in your Christian walk, and spiritual maturity exercised will be your true test of humility. If someone walks up to you and slaps your face, would you respond in love pushing aside your anger and your pride? Jesus in scripture did, and He calls us to do this as well. Jesus maintained His humility throughout His ministry and even to the finished work at the cross.

I have literally experienced betrayal by at least three significant people within the church that I brought in as friends and whom I have served in humility and when they turned around and tore me apart, each and every time, I chose humility. I chose to give it to God rather than try to defend myself or pay them back with harmful words or actions. Let me tell you something, it's not easy, it's never easy, but when you see God handle it for you each time it happens, it does get a bit easier.

In the book of Luke, Jesus was humbly met by Simon of Cyrene who assisted Jesus in carrying the cross to Calvary. Jesus maintained humility in love for the soldiers that strung Him upon the cross and gambled His clothes, yet Jesus focused on praying to God the Father... "Father forgive them for they do not know what they do."

Being humble is not about focusing on yourself, rather, the test is if you can focus on others despite your feelings and your pride. We are called to do as Jesus did, as we are to do only what we see our Heavenly Father do!

Apostle Paul wrote over thirteen epistles demonstrating humility. Paul's summarized message to us is to run this race of life with endurance and to do that we *need* humility. We must push forward having the courage to finish this race of life strong and obtain the prize...pushing for our "crowns," not to selfishly keep for ourselves but to be able to humbly cast our crowns at the feet of the KING of kings, and LORD of lords, Jesus.

Scripture talks a lot about being humble. This is not only to keep us from being arrogant, but also, if we are too proud to accept help from someone else, we block God from blessing us with what we asked Him for. God sometimes uses people to do His blessing. We are moved by His Spirit, and when He needs to bless you, He will move the heart of another believer to do His blessing; receive it! Allow yourself to receive. Never be too proud to accept the gift God sends you through the hands of someone else. He will return a blessing to them as well in return for their obedience in blessing you. Do not be surprised at times God will even use your enemies to bless you.

Daniel 10:12 "don't be afraid. God has heard your prayers ever since the first day you decided to humble yourself in order to gain understanding."

If you want God to hear your prayers, humble yourself. Don't be afraid, because you're not doing it in *your* strength, but trust in Him to make a way. Many times, we hold back from believing or asking God for too much because we want to protect His reputation or we don't want to get let down, but God doesn't need your help, and that is when He gets the most glory, in the big things! Ask big! Pray to Him and ask Him to step in and do what only He can do. If you want God to hear and respond to your prayers, you've got to humble yourself and believe that He is the Almighty God.

Zechariah 4:6 "Not by strength or by might, but by my Spirit."

Sure, we can do certain things, and He wants us to do what is within our ability, but there comes a time when you realize that life is totally out of your control and there is nothing that you can do in your own might to change your circumstances. You can even pray and cry out to God, day and night, but if you are proud and take responsibility for all your achievements, God will not answer your prayers.

Job 35:12 "They cry for help, but God doesn't answer, for they are proud and evil."

God will bring us through things in order to reveal Himself to us; to show His power and to prove that He is in control. If you are full of pride and believe that you are where you are and have what you have because of your own efforts, God will show you otherwise.

Have you ever noticed how the times you're feeling down about yourself, people around you tend to counter that and fill you with praises of your good qualities and the good you've done? And in the same way, when you speak so big and mighty about yourself, people around you might say things to kind of bring you down a notch or two? Well surprise, it's scriptural!

Matthew 23:12 "Whoever makes himself great will be humbled, and whoever humbles himself will be made great."

You never want to be the one to brag on yourself or sing your own praises. You don't have to prove yourself to anyone. If you're always elevating yourself, you don't leave anyone else the chance to. The gist of humility is saying less, which is actually exercising more through the character of silence.

Proverbs 25:7 "It is better to be asked to take a higher position than to be told to give your place to someone more important."

How embarrassing! Seriously, I would much rather take a seat all the way in the back of the building and be asked to come forward than seat myself front and center and be asked to move back for someone more important.

Proverbs 27:2 "Let other people praise you — even strangers; never do it yourself."

I mean, it's just cringy to brag on yourself. Leave it up to God to exalt you. Believe me, He's much better at it. He has a way of highlighting the best of you, and you won't ever have to say a word about it. You don't have to explain it to anyone, simply do what is just, show love, and He will reward you openly.

Micah 6:8 "the Lord has told us what is good. What He requires of us is this: to do what is just, to show constant love, and to live in <u>humble</u> fellowship with our God."

Live in humble fellowship with God. Don't ever consider yourself a better Christian because of your own works. Never feel as though you're better than anyone, for any reason, but especially not because of your faith. God loves a sinner on the street just as much as He loves you or me or the pastor at the church. You are of no use to God if you consider yourself better than anyone else.

Proverbs 3:34 "He has no use for conceited people, but shows favor to those who are humble."
Job 5:11 "Yes, it is God who raises the humble and gives joy to all who mourn."

Your humility will bring you the favor and joy of the Lord. God is good! So, turn away from your sins and trust in His goodness. He is on our side! I see so many people who have got the wrong idea of God, His love and how He operates. They treat Him like the enemy because they expect Him to be good but blame Him for every bad thing they've ever experienced, not knowing that the devil is, in fact, the god of this world. He was banished from Heaven and is here, with us, causing confusion. But if they only knew if they turned to God and walked with Him *through* the persecutions of the enemy, God would bring them out and bless them.

How to Deal: *With the Present*

Job 22:21 "make peace with God and stop treating Him like an enemy;
if you do then He will bless you. Accept the teaching He gives; keep His
Words in your heart. Yes, you must humbly return to God and put an
end to all the evil that is done in your house."

     Turn back to God, with the right perspective. Give
Him a chance to prove His Word, His promise! Accept the
teaching He gives. Obey His commands and He will bless
you; He will save you from destruction. Turning to Satan in
distain for God is just accepting an endless cycle to suffering.
You will still face suffering in your walk with the Lord, of
course, we all do, even Jesus did; but with God there is an
end, there is a blessing in sight.

Malachi 4:1 "The Lord Almighty says, 'The day is coming when all
proud and evil people will burn like straw. — But for you who obey Me,
My saving power will rise on you.'"
Zephaniah 2:3 "Turn to the Lord, all you humble people of the land,
who obey His commands. Do what is right, and humble yourselves before
the Lord. Perhaps you will escape punishment on the day when the Lord
shows His anger."

     Excuse me, sir. Um, burn like straw? Yikes. Take it
from me, you want to heed this warning before you find out
for yourself. I never thought I would learn such a hard lesson
in such a devastating way, I always thought, *it would never*

happen to me, but it was out of my control. I never even saw it coming. But it's in those hard times that you grow the most. You learn things you never could have learned otherwise. I was too stubborn. I was stuck in my ways. I didn't want to grow; I was content.

But God will take us to rock bottom to break us, in order to get us to our potential. I had no choice but to look up. I had no choice but to turn to Him. I had lost everything. Everything I loved most in life, because at that time, as sad as it is, it wasn't even people. My possessions meant absolutely everything to me. And they were all gone in an instant.

Ecclesiastes 2:18 "Nothing that I had worked for and earned meant a thing to me, because I knew that I would have to leave it to my successor."

I get that now; I have been humbled by my struggles. Material things don't matter, they don't last. Sure, they're nice, and I'm not saying I don't still desire to have nice things, I do, but I don't live for them anymore. I know that there's something greater in life than just having the nicest car parked outside of the nicest house with the nicest décor and clothes and shoes and designer bags inside. I like all those things, but even greater than all that is the person I became when all those things were stripped away.

285

How to Deal: *With the Present*

2 Samuel 22:28 "You save the humble, but your eyes are on the haughty to bring them low."

If you think you're all that, hunny, God will bring you down! If your only concern is yourself and you think your way is the only right way and you judge everyone else because they have their own way of doing things, babyy…you're gonna learn today!

Proverbs 11:2 "People who are proud will soon be disgraced. It is wiser to be modest."

Don't try to make yourself seem better or more important than anyone else, you're not. Don't try to impress people with lies or exaggerations of who you really are or by bringing others down, just be you.

Proverbs 29:25 "It is dangerous to be concerned with what others think of you, but if you trust in the Lord, you are safe."

People's opinions of you are none of your business. Trust in what He says about you and how He sees you. Trust that His thoughts about you are true and without selfish reasoning. Trust that He made you perfectly, you! Trust in the Lord in humility and you will be safe. Humility means knowing that even if He never blesses us with a material physical blessing, we understand that His love for us is enough, His protection is enough, His plans for us are enough, His sacrifice for us was enough.

Psalm 63:3-4 "Because Your steadfast love is better than life, my lips will praise You. So I will bless You as long as I live; in Your Name I will lift up my hands."

No matter our ignorance, the Lord never gives up on us, however He is going to return, and I ask you, have you accepted Jesus Christ as your Lord and Savior? If not, I urge you to humbly reconsider, because we do not know the moment, the second, or the hour of Jesus' return.

Turn to Him even in the midst of chaos and pain. Trust the process, God changes caterpillars into butterflies and coal into diamonds using time and pressure. He's working on you, too. Be patient and trust in Him; remember, peace and joy do not come from the absence of struggle and conflict. Learn from the process, allow the presence of God to create a stillness within you that is greater than what is going on around you. God has not forgotten you. If you're committing your steps to Him, He is ordering them — whether you realize it or not.

Chapter 9

Prepare for your Breakthrough

Prepare yourself for your new season. Even before you see it begin to manifest, before you have the means to make it happen, before you even fully believe you are capable of doing it or achieving it. Do what you can do now so that when an opportunity presents or a door opens, you're not scurrying around trying to get your thoughts together at the last second.

Habakkuk 2:2-3 "Write down clearly on tablets what I reveal to you, so that it can be read at a glance. Put it in writing, because it is not yet time for it to come true. But the time is coming quickly, and what I show

Prepare for Your Breakthrough

you will come true. It may seem slow in coming, but wait for it; it will certainly take place, and it will not be delayed."

You've got to wait for God's time; but when it comes, you better be prepared. Think about it, if you're expecting God to bless you with a million-dollar check in the mail, but you don't know how to manage the three-hundred dollars a week you're making now, not to mention you don't even have a bank account set up to cash the check, why would God ever send it? He won't send something He knows you're not prepared to receive. Manage what you have now, and He will bless you with greater!

Matthew 25:21 "You have been faithful in managing small amounts, so I will put you in charge of large amounts."

If you're expecting God to bless you with a child, but you don't have the patience to drive a mile down the road without cussing everyone out, how do you expect Him to bless you with a precious little screaming, crying, puking, messy, whiny, trouble making, back-talking child?

Be prepared for what you want! If you have an idea for a business but are lacking the resources to bring it to fruition and are trusting in God to make a way, you should have your business model worked out and ready to go so that if He were to drop a check in the mail this minute in the amount you need, you'd be able to hit the ground running! I can *want* to be a business owner all day and night but if I don't educate myself now on what it takes, then sure, I can start a business, no problem, but it'll crash and burn in no time.

Proverbs 19:2 "Desire without knowledge is not good – how much more will hasty feet miss the way!"

In life, you're going to have ups and downs. You're going to fail, but how much more likely are we to fail if we move too hastily? We must learn *before* we leap. Envision it as if it were happening now! Don't think of it as a waste of time because, "who knows if it'll ever happen" rather, think of the time invested as an investment into your future. If you have the faith to believe that God can make a way, then move forward in that faith knowing that you are preparing for the inevitable move of God to make it happen.

Isaiah 43:19 Watch for the new thing I am going to do. It is happening already – you can see it now! I will make a road through the wilderness."

It is happening already! You don't have to see it moving to know that God is working. God is active in areas and realms beyond our own understanding. We don't see the air we breathe, yet we know that it's still there and available for our next breath. Keep breathing. Always be sharpening your skills. Whatever God has placed in your heart, whatever God has called you to do, be prepared as if you were expecting it to happen tomorrow. You will not know the exact time God will move, but if you're not prepared, if you're not ready to receive, you could miss your opportunity.

1 Peter 1:13 "So, then, have your minds ready for action. Keep alert and set your hope completely on the blessing which will be given you when Jesus Christ is revealed."

Release control. You have no power over when it will happen, so trust in God's timing and praise Him that it's on the way. Keep your hope on the blessing that is coming. Imagine your vision happening and magnify your praise not your problems. Thank God for His favor in your life from a place of completion, say, "Lord, thank you for delivering me from this problem I'm facing." rather than, "I have this problem, God, please work it out." Speak from a place of faith that it's already done.

Romans 4:17 "who gives life to the dead and calls those things which do not exist as though they did."

How to Deal: *With the Present*

God brings dead things to life. You must announce and declare the year of God's favor. What you say and pray for may not be true at the time, but you can still announce freedom from things holding you back and boldly announce favor IS coming, and your situation IS turning around. It may not look like it now, people might think you're *crazy* – who cares, say it anyway!

For example: I am blessed, favored, and will serve the Lord my God; I am healthy and prosperous, successful in all things that I touch.

Proverbs 3:5 "Trust in the Lord with all your heart. Never rely on what you think you know.
Proverbs 3:6 "Remember the Lord in everything you do, and He will show you the right way."

This season was not necessarily brought on by the devil; the Holy Spirit will lead you into the wilderness for you to be tempted, tested, and to strengthen your faith to prepare you for your new, breakthrough season. If you don't pass the test, just like in the natural life, you'll have to take it again. But the good news is that God will use this suffering to reveal His glory and to bring us out of our comfort zone, out of our contentment and bless us with the future we hope for. He uses all things, good and bad, for our good.

Prepare for Your Breakthrough

Romans 8:18 "I consider that what we suffer at this present time cannot be compared at all with the glory that is going to be revealed to us."

These are His promises! Don't just hear them, use them to prepare! This should motivate you to be ready as if what you're asking for will come tomorrow. He says never rely on what you think you know, the time is coming quickly, and it will *certainly* take place, He says it's happening already, I will make a road in the wilderness, He says He will show you the right way; so, get ready!!

2 Peter 3:14-15 "And so, my friends, as you wait for that Day, do your best to be pure and faultless in God's sight and to be at peace with Him. Look on our Lord's patience as the opportunity He is giving you to be saved, just as our dear friend Paul wrote to you, using the wisdom that God gave him."

You may think that God is taking forever to answer you, but the truth is, His patience and His grace is allowing you the time to get it together!! So, the quicker you get it together, the quicker He can bless you!

2 Peter 3:8-9 "There is no difference in the Lord's sight between one day and a thousand years; to Him the two are the same. The Lord is not slow to do what He has promised, as some think. Instead, He is patient with you, because He does not want anyone to be destroyed, but wants all to turn away from their sins."

He is giving us plenty of time to get right and turn away from our sins and be washed clean. He wants to give us a fresh start, no matter what we've done! You can be a new creation in Christ!

Ephesians 4:22-32 "So get rid of your old self, which made you live as you used to – the old self that was being destroyed by its deceitful desires. Your hearts and minds must be made completely new, and you must put on the new self, which is created in God's likeness and reveals itself in the true life that is upright and holy. No more lying, then! Each of you must tell the truth to the other believer, because we are all members together in the body of Christ. If you become angry, do not let your anger lead you into sin, and do not stay angry all day. Don't give the devil a chance. If you used to rob, you must stop robbing and start working, in order to earn an honest living for yourself and to be able to help the poor. Do not use harmful words, but only helpful words, the kind that build up and provide what is needed, so that what you say will do good to those who hear you. And do not make God's Holy Spirit sad; for the Spirit is God's mark of ownership on you, a guarantee that the Day will come when God will set you free. Get rid of all bitterness, passion and anger. No more shouting or insults, no more hateful feelings of any sort. Instead, be kind and tenderhearted to one another, and forgive one another, as God has forgiven you through Christ."

Prepare for Your Breakthrough

If you're not prepared, your blessing could pass right by you. That's why He will not bless you now, because He knows you'll miss it. God *wants* to bless you! You think you're waiting on Him, but He's been waiting on you! Do good, turn away from your sins, make an honest living, bless others, be kind, love one another – these are all things that are pleasing to God, and when He is prepared to bless you, He will bless you according to what you have done, so what *have* you done? Now is the time, it's not too late, get prepared.

Revelations 22:12-14 "'Listen!' says Jesus, 'I am coming soon! I will bring My rewards with Me, to give each one according to what he has done. I am the first and the last, the beginning and the end.' Happy are those who wash their robes clean and so have the right to eat the fruit from the tree of life and to go through the gates into the city."

I'm really trying to get you all to understand that His Word is His promise, it is His covenant, and it cannot be broken. As long as you do your part, He *will* do His, He has to! Even if you might not believe it just yet, what do you have to lose?! You might be nice to somebody and get no reward for it? Trusting in His Word is a win-win situation! You cannot lose!

How to Deal: *With the Present*

James 1:22 "Do not deceive yourselves by just listening to His Word; instead, put it into practice."

So don't sit around waiting on God to move, put His Word into practice! Don't wonder if it's God's will for you to succeed, you know His Word, you know His promises! Claim them! Whether you're waiting on a blessing of healing – He wants to heal you; salvation – He wants you and your family and friends to be saved; finances – He wants us to prosper and have the ability to bless others; restoration – He will restore double what was lost, or you may be up against someone in court or the court itself – y'all, equip yourself with the Holy Spirit, He's got you! The Bible says in those instances when you are confronted you won't even have to worry about what you will say, and what you say will not be refuted.

Luke 12:11 "When they bring you to be tried in the synagogues or before governors or rulers, do not be worried about how you will defend yourself or what you will say. For the Holy Spirit will teach you at that time what you should say."
Acts 6:10 "But the Spirit gave Stephen such wisdom that when he spoke, they could not refute him."

Put His Word into practice! It doesn't matter what your situation looks like, if God has promised you something,

296

nobody can stop it! Keep putting in the work, push through to the goal, pray it out and keep the faith. Whatever your situation may be, be alert, and trust that no matter what happens or how it looks, God's got a plan for you.

1 Corinthians 16:13 "Be alert, stand firm in the faith, be brave, be strong. Do all your work in love."

His Word says that when He comes, He will bless each of us according to what we've done. Now, whether you've got a blessing of health, favor, and prosperity on the way or whether you've got a blessing of correction, pain, and suffering on the way is all dependent on what you choose to do and how you choose to live from this day forward. How will God want to bless you? You won't get a warning when your time is coming, don't wait until it's too late.

1 Thessalonians 5:2-4 "For you yourselves know very well that the Day of the Lord will come as a thief comes at night. When people say, 'Everything is quiet and safe,' then suddenly destruction will hit them! It will come as suddenly as the pains that come upon a woman in labor, and people will not escape. But you, friends, are not in the darkness, and the Day should not take you by surprise as a thief."

He doesn't expect us to be perfect. Of course, He wants you to live right, but He wants to bless you and anoint you where you are right now at your dirtiest point, as Samuel discovered David. God doesn't anoint finished work; He anoints you so that you can finish the work! You're relevant because you've got the anointing AND the dust. You may not be perfect now, but come out of your darkness, and receive the Light, so that He can use you, and bless you, and save you on the day He comes.

Matthew 24:43-44&46 "If the owner of a house knew the time when the thief would come, you can be sure that he would stay awake and not let the thief break into his house. So then, you also must always be ready, because the Son of Man will come at an hour when you are not expecting Him. – How happy that servant is if his master finds him doing [right] when he comes home."

God does not warn us to give us time to get it together at the last minute, to put on a "show" of righteousness. He wants to come and see that you have been living a *life* of kindness, goodness, and love. So, get ready now, do something good for someone today. Help someone other than your family, other than yourself! Smile at the people you pass by today. Give someone a hug or a kind, encouraging word. Make kindness a lifestyle. The little things matter!

Prepare for Your Breakthrough

Maybe you have been living a generous, helpful, kind, and loving life for years and it seems you're always helping others, but nobody is ever there for you, don't get discouraged. Never stop doing good. Your kindness and generosity are doing more than you know, even if you don't feel appreciated. Don't give up.

Luke 12:35-36, 40 & 45-46 "Be ready for whatever comes, dressed for action and with your lamps lit, like servants who are waiting for their master to come back from a wedding feast. When he comes and knocks, they will open the door for him at once. And you, too, must be ready, because the Son of Man will come at an hour when you are not expecting Him. – But if that servant says to himself that his master is taking a long time to come back and if he begins to beat the other servants, both the men and the women, and eats and drinks and gets drunk, then the master will come back one day when the servant does not expect him and at a time he does not know. The master will cut him in pieces and make him share the fate of the disobedient."

You haven't come this far to give up now. It may seem hard, but your pain is what defines your purpose. Not everyone was called to be a comforter. What God placed in you was hidden, and you may feel that you have been undervalued and that your talents have been overlooked and underappreciated, but that's where God makes leaders.

How to Deal: *With the Present*

God is about to pull the curtain back on your gifts and hidden talents. The treasure He's been establishing in you through the process of pain, tears, and prayer, is about to be revealed; this is that moment. You had to be hidden because He had to be sure that your character matched your calling. They couldn't see you because God hid you, to see that you don't need validation from outside sources. Be secure in who He created you to be. God is looking for people to serve when no one is looking because if you can serve when no one is looking He will give you favor when everyone's looking.

Never deny or turn away from your calling. Nothing moves until the one God chose, comes. Ideas, businesses, companies won't work until you show up! You are a key to the entire system! When you are in the presence of authority, you rise.

And in the meantime, remember, there is purpose where you are. While you are preparing for where you *want* to be, don't neglect the very purpose God has for you while you are where you are.

Part 3

How to Deal: *With Your Future*

Chapter 10

Remain Humble

People will cheer you on from about a 0 to a 7 – anything beyond that, people get insecure and try to stop or block your success. They want to see you succeed, just not *too* much, not more than them. When God elevates you, people will come against you, expect it.

Humility means that if or when someone smacks you in the face, comes against you with lies and false allegations, you don't hit back, you don't defend yourself. Jesus didn't defend Himself when people questioned His authority. He didn't hit back when He was being beat and spit on and hung up on the cross to be left for dead. When people questioned His authority, He responded by asking, "Who do you say I am?" He had already proven by example exactly who He is, He doesn't need to defend Himself, and neither do we.

Remain Humble

God is our defender, and as Christians, we should be living life as an example of who we are, so that if someone were to lie on you, you don't have to defend or explain yourself, simply answer, "Who do you say that I am?" Essentially, what you are saying is, who have I *proven* myself to be? Is this accusation in line with my character as you know it? From there, you give it to God to defend you and make it right, and He will.

God has elevated my husband and I pretty significantly at this point in my writing this book, and it's funny because the first time in my life I got a little taste of success outside of God, before the fire, I let it get to my head; I was a little out of touch. Now, it's almost funny to see people react to seeing us where we're at now, because they expect a different "type" of person for what we look like. People expect us to be snobby or be rude, but I came from nothing, and I will always be that same little girl running around barefoot around the campfire in the dirt, no matter where I go or what I have.

It's to the point that when my husband and I help people for free without expectation for anything in return, people look so hard to find the angle. It saddens me, however, that simply acting in a way God has called us to act with one another is so rare that when people do see it, they feel threatened, defensive, and push it away.

I never in my life want to get to the place where I think I'm better than everyone and above everything. No matter what God blesses me with, I never want to lose sight of caring for others – at every level – with the kindness and compassion we all deserve.

Don't forget what you learned in the wilderness. Sometimes I find myself desperately thankful after my prayers are answered, but then I stop praying. Eventually I stop praising Him for what He did, and the next time something troublesome comes up, I begin to question if God is even real, forgetting how undeniably real He was to me in that last instance. To be completely honest, I'm facing that this very minute. But I know God will show up and come through at precisely the right time if I just continue to focus on others and let Him focus on me.

It has taken this season of humility and all-time lows to grow a genuine care and compassion for others that I have never had before. It's not always easy, but it is something that I desperately strive to hold onto.

Remain Humble

Sometimes being nice to everyone all the time is exhausting, especially, for me, when I feel it's not even being appreciated or acknowledged; sometimes people are just flat out rude and disrespectful!

I had an incident recently when I was in the store wearing a Christian t-shirt which, sidebar, I feel like every time I wear a Christian shirt of any kind I always get tempted somewhere, by someone, to let my crazy show! The shirt said, "I'm God's favorite!" on the front, and on the back, it said, "...and so are you!" so while I'm walking through the store and feeling the joy of the Lord, there was a woman stopped with her cart in the aisle next to me and an older woman coming up behind her toward me. I shoot her a smile as I press myself into the clothing, so she has room to pass through. She shoots back a smug pity grin and as she gets up next to me, she looks me up and down and says with disgust, "*You're* not God's favorite, *God* doesn't have favorites." And continues past me.

Look...the fact that homegirl didn't get her cart kicked in was a testament to my salvation that day. I smiled a genuine smile to myself and continued out of the store. I tell my husband in the car and he said he liked to think that she looked back and saw the back of the shirt and felt conviction for being so rude. I like to believe that's true because I would hate for her to continue going around speaking to people that way and making assumptions but either way, it was a blessing for me just to see God come through me in that way; it was certainly a new experience for me to respond that way!

I'm thinking, *Lord, if she only knew how I used to be. She doesn't even know what it takes for me to be nice to her little ungrateful face right now. The old me would have at the very least cussed her out and went about my day.*

But it's easy when I remember what He's done for me; that was no coincidence. I remember that He's saved me once, and He'll do it again. He brought me through this season to teach me what I desperately needed to learn, and I don't want to give Him any reason to think it's a lesson I need to learn again.

I have learned to have compassion on those who are hurting, even if that hurt manifests itself in a nasty way towards me. I never want to forget all He's done for me or take it for granted. If this were the only result of the season I came through, it would be enough. I want to be a good representation of Jesus to the best of my ability. If someone hates me because of Jesus, I'm cool; if someone hates Jesus because of *me,* it's a problem. I never want the lessons I learned through the struggles to be wasted, and I never want to have to learn them again!

2 Corinthians 6:1-2 "In our work together with God, then, we beg you who have received God's grace not to let it be wasted. Hear what God says, 'When the time came for Me to show you favor, I heard you; when the day arrived for Me to save you, I helped you.' Listen! This is the hour to receive God's favor; today is the day to be saved."

The God of the universe has shown me grace and favor. So go ahead, come against me! Be nasty towards me! Lie on me! I don't care anymore. You won't get a reaction from me. Grace and peace unto you, sister. God gives us His grace as a gift, not to keep, but to extend to others. Don't come out of your mess only to revert to your old ways. Don't quit doing good now that you've got what you asked for. Accept what you've learned, that was a blessing in itself! Praise Him for it with a thankful and joyful heart! Show Him your gratitude by continuing to live right as a good example of God's work. Maintain a reverence for the God who brought you out and delivered you from devastation and drought, far above your distain for nasty, hurtful people. We should come out of this as a positive representative of God's goodness and His work within us. We should live as an example that He would be proud to have representing Him.

How to Deal: *With Your Future*

Zephaniah 3:7 "I thought that then My people would have reverence for Me and accept My discipline, that they would never forget the lesson I taught them. But soon they were behaving as badly as ever."

Don't be the type of representation of God who goes around telling other believers that they are less than worthy or doing it wrong. They don't need *your* correction. If they need correction, God is big enough to do it. He doesn't need your abrasive "help." I mean, come on, we're confronting complete strangers for feeling *too* loved by God now? What is this? And yet people, even believers, wonder why they *stay* miserable. Don't think that God won't take you back through the same old mess. You don't want to give God any reason to take you back into the same wilderness for the same thing. God uses these lessons to keep us from the path of evil.

Job 36:21 "Be careful not to turn to evil; your suffering was sent you to keep you from it."

God didn't send you through troubles to torture you, it was a correction of love, it was to keep you from doing what was wrong and teach you what's right. Grace is right, mercy is right, it's a part of His work through our suffering, to reveal to us His example of unconditional love, mercy, and grace. Don't ignore this teaching point, it's a part of the process. Receive it from Him and give it to others. Just as we

Remain Humble

do as parents, when our kids make mistakes or mess up, we correct them. There are consequences they won't like, but we come around in the end to show them love and grace. They may not like the punishment, but they're better for it in the end, and so are we.

Proverbs 3:11-12 "My child, when the Lord corrects you, pay close attention and take it as a warning. The Lord corrects those He loves, as parents correct a child of whom they are proud."

The discipline of the Lord is the other side of His grace. If we can grasp the intent behind His discipline, we can begin to cherish it for what it is, His love for us, as His children. God is not evil or insensitive. He corrects us because He loves us. He wants us to be better – for Him, for each other, for our loved ones and for ourselves. He corrects us to bring us closer, He wants us to come faultless into His presence. He sacrificed His own Son for it!

Colossians 1:21-22 "At one time you were far away from God and were His enemies because of the evil things you did and thought. But now, by means of the physical death of His Son, God has made you His friends, in order to bring you, holy, pure, and faultless, into His presence."

His desire is to bring us, *holy, pure and faultless* into His presence. He is at work in us. Remember all He's done for you when you were helpless in your own strength. Devote your life to Him. Accept His correction. Look outside of yourself! Only in Him are we holy, pure, and faultless in His presence. We can do nothing outside of Him; anything we attempt in our own strength is useless.

Psalm 127:1 "If the Lord does not build the house, the work of the builders is useless."

Build your future on Him; Christ is your foundation for all that you build and all that you do. Any builder knows that the foundation is the most important part of a building. In the same way, Christ is the most crucial component of anything we do. We should always take it to Him first, consult with Him, pray about it, thank Him for it, include Him in it.

1 Corinthians 3:11 "For God has already placed Jesus Christ as the one and only foundation, and no other foundation can be laid."

The foundation is the strength of a building. If you have a weak foundation, you have a weak structure. In the same way, if we attempt to be the foundation of our own stuff, it is sure to fail. Don't try to take it on yourself. Sometimes we get on such a steady stream of success and begin to think we are the ones who are being successful; but it's still God, it's only God.

Galatians 3:3-4 "How can you be so foolish! You began by God's Spirit; do you now want to finish by your own power? Did all your experience mean nothing at all? Surely it meant something!"

Paul reminds us that our Christian life, our new season, the blessings we are walking in today, all began in the Spirit by faith alone, and being made perfect by the flesh indicates trying to achieve perfection through our own efforts and thus, taking the credit for ourselves and that is all wrong. It's through Him, it was always Him, and He will continue to come through for you. He's coming through on His promises, all He asks is for your respect. Don't you dare take the credit for what He's done for you. Give Him the glory He's due. If you've achieved greatness, it's alright to boast, but boast about what the *Lord* has done through you, not what you have done for yourself.

2 Corinthians 10:17 "But as the scripture says, 'Whoever wants to boast must boast about what the Lord has done.'"

He makes us successful so that His Name would be praised, and He would get the glory. Don't you dare take the credit for yourself; He doesn't ask for much, but He gives us everything. He gives us what we could never attain on our own. Put some respekk on His name! I am absolutely sure that I can do nothing without Him.

Malachi 2:5 "In My covenant I promised them life and well-being, and this is what I gave them, so that they might respect Me."

    Respect Him by being a delightful representation of Him, of His love. Help and give to others. Be a blessing to others. Don't think that just because you've been blessed that suddenly you're better than anyone else; that's not what all this was for. Even if God elevates you to the highest position you could ever dream of reaching, you must always consider others better than yourself.

Philippians 2:3 "Don't do anything from selfish ambition or from cheap desire to boast, but be humble toward one another, always considering others better than yourselves."

    The point of considering others better than yourself is not to diminish you as a person or your achievements, but if we all treated others better and considered others better than ourselves, how great would the world be? If we treated the janitor with the same respect as the CEO, so to speak. That is how we should think, because it is the Lord who promotes. Both janitor and CEO work hard, both struggle, both show up to work, both have a family to provide for, both have ego and emotions, and both have something to offer the world; both men have value and should be valued. But often we are more interested in lending a hand to the CEO who has plenty of staff to support him, than picking up a broom to help the janitor. Regardless of the position the Lord has given you, you are never above accepting humble duties. Pick up the broom.

Romans 12:16 "Have the same concern for everyone. Do not be proud, but accept humble duties. Do not think of yourselves as wise."

"Do not think of yourselves as wise." Why? Because wisdom is not our own. It is the Lord who gives us wisdom. Contrary to what granny says, it is not age that makes us wise, but God alone. His Spirit gives us wisdom, His Spirit enables us to get promoted, to write the book, to start the business, to achieve success. Give glory to whom glory is due.

Job 32:8-9 "But it is the Spirit of Almighty God that comes to us and gives us wisdom. It is not growing old that makes us wise or helps us to know what is right."

Even Jesus, Himself, fully man, and fully God, did not try to remain equal with God. He did not consider Himself better than or equal to, He chose humility until His last breath. Even hanging on the cross in between a murderer and a thief, yet never once exalted Himself, faultless and without sin, above the others.

Philippians 2:6-11 "[Jesus] always had the nature of God, but He did not think that by force He should try to remain equal with God. Instead of this, of His own free will He gave up all He had, and took the nature of a servant. He became like a human being and appeared in human likeness. He was humble and walked the path of obedience all the way to death – His death on the cross. For this reason God raised Him to the highest place above and gave Him the name that is greater than any other name. And so, in honor of the name of Jesus all beings in Heaven, on earth, and in the world below will fall on their knees, and all will openly proclaim that Jesus Christ is Lord, to the glory of God the Father."

    Jesus gave God the glory and took the most humble position and sacrificed His life and He was rewarded with the greatest reward. God rewards humility. You may feel like a punk, but the lower He finds you, the higher God brings you, and He will reward you with far greater than the lowest low you have ever felt. So, if you're feeling low, trust Him. He sees where you are, He's got you, and He will guide you through.

Remain Humble

Proverbs 3:5-6 "Trust in the Lord with all your heart. Never rely on what you think you know. Remember the Lord in everything you do, and He will show you the right way."

Don't let your suffering be in vain, His whole purpose was to leave you humble and living a purposeful life. You're the same person now as you were then, just with different circumstances. Remain humble with what God has given you. Continue to pray, continue to praise Him for every little thing He did for you along the way. Don't forget your journey.

Zephaniah 3:12 "I will leave there a humble and lowly people, who will come to Me for help. [Those] who survive will do no wrong to anyone, tell no lies, nor try to deceive. They will be prosperous and secure, afraid of no one."

Again, there is a purpose to your struggle. He wants you to come out of this mess prosperous, secure, and afraid of no one. If you are righteous and honest, He will help you and protect you! When you see the way He comes in and saves you, you won't fear every little bump in the road. You can trust that He's watching, He sees you, and at the right moment He will step in and help you.

How to Deal: *With Your Future*

Proverbs 2:7-8 He provides help and protection for those who are righteous and honest. He protects those who treat others fairly, and guards those who are devoted to Him."

Don't get corrupted by your status. Remain righteous and honest. Treat others fairly. Most importantly, remain devoted to God. Be His reflection here on earth. Love the poor just as you did when you yourself were poor. Don't stop volunteering now that you're suddenly so busy managing all your blessings, if you allow your blessings to become a distraction, God will strip them right away.

Daniel 4:27 "follow my advice. Stop sinning, do what is right, and be merciful to the poor. Then you will continue to be prosperous."
Proverbs 27:7 "When you are full, you will refuse honey, but when you are hungry, even bitter food tastes sweet."

Don't refuse what's good because you think you've made it, you've got enough, you've arrived. God wants to continue to bless you. Don't refuse what you know is good. Continue to obey His Word and the rest of your life will be long and prosperous. This is a lifestyle, not a one-off blessing. We should live a life of obedience to the Lord, it is in our best interest to do so!

Remain Humble

Proverbs 22:4 "Obey the Lord, be humble, and you will get riches, honor, and a long life.

EXCUSE ME? I'm sorry, isn't this what most people are chasing? I mean, if we're being honest. Sooo…if we obey the Lord in the simple things He asks of us, and be humble, He promises us riches? Honor? And a long life?

It actually makes more sense, if you think about it, even beyond faith. God is the Creator of all things – you, me and the entire universe. He knows what is best for us, He knows what kind of lifestyle will keep us around for a long time. So, beyond faith in God, it's faith in the Creator – the manufacturer, if you will. If I want to know how to keep a Lamborghini running for as long as possible, I'm going to consult the Lamborghini dealer, I'm not going to take it to Jiffy Lube. In the same way, if I want to know how to achieve success in life and live long, I'm going to listen to the plans of God, not man. He brought you out once, you've seen the blessing, don't allow the temptation of man or yourself to lead you astray.

Job 36:16-18 "God brought you out of trouble, and let you enjoy security; your table was piled high with food. But now you are being punished as you deserve. Be careful not to let bribes deceive you, or riches lead you astray."

How to Deal: *With Your Future*

You strive for more riches, but God is your source, He is your wealth, without Him you have nothing. In Him there is joy. Don't let Him be replaced with material things; they do not compare.

Job 22:25-30 "Let Almighty God be your gold, and let Him be silver, piled high for you. Then you will always trust in God and find that He is the source of your joy. When you pray, He will answer you, and you will keep the vows you made. You will succeed in all you do, and light will shine on your path God brings down the proud and saves the humble. He will rescue you if you are innocent, if what you do is right."

Keep the vows you made out of desperation before you had it all. Don't be corrupted by your blessings. Continue to turn to Him for all your needs. Your resources are not your source, God is your only source; respect Him as such. Keep God in first place in your life, above all else. Don't get lost in your new life.

Zechariah 10:2 "So the people wander about like lost sheep. They are in trouble because they have no leader."

Stay out of trouble! This season was intended to build character; continue to obey God's commands and keep His teachings; all that He asks of you is to love Him and love one another as you love yourself! That's it! Don't let anyone persuade you otherwise. Often, those at the top can tend to be callous. Be careful who you let in your circle. The people you surround yourself with have a major impact on you, your behavior and where you're going. You may have to end some friendships.

1 Corinthians 15:33 "Bad companions ruin good character."

There is now a power in you to be a leader. Don't conform to others and their bad character because that's the standard. You set the standard. God gives us the power in our inner selves; use it! Maintain your roots and foundation in love, regardless of the actions of others. Set the standard; be the example.

Ephesians 3:16-18 "I ask God from the wealth of His glory to give you power through His Spirit to be strong in your inner selves, and I pray that Christ will make His home in your hearts through faith. I pray that you may have your roots and foundation in love."

Chapter 11

Prepare for Disaster

Sometimes, as believers, we think that if we are right with God and behave well enough, we will be free from trials. In fact, I've heard it said recently that God does not send or allow suffering in order to bring about His purpose. This is simply not true. We can see proof of that all throughout the Bible, let's look at Job specifically; Satan needed God's permission to come against Job. God allowed it. God set the limits. God decided when it was to end.

To walk with God is not to be free from storms. That is a terribly dangerous theology. Don't ever think that now that you're out of the wilderness and walking close with God, praying, and reading your Bible every day, that makes you immune to disaster. Excuse me, but if Jesus' own disciples were beheaded, skinned alive, boiled in oil – um hello, if Jesus Himself was whipped, beaten, spit on, plucked by the beard and crucified, what makes us as Christians think we'll never face trouble again if we try to be good? We could never be good enough! We have seen trouble before, we have made it out, and guess what, we'll see it again!

Ecclesiastes 1:9 "What has happened before will happen again. What has been done before will be done again."

God does not keep us from ever experiencing trouble again. He does, however, walk us through it. He doesn't remove us from the sea, He parts it so we can get through it easier.

These guidelines I have laid out are a tool to use continually throughout life. You should always be prepared for a disaster; because once it comes, if you're not prepared to look beyond it and put your faith in God to get you through, you're already destroyed. Expect more trials, because they're coming! But if you're prepared for the "test" and you pass, you're already on your way to your next season.

How to Deal: *With Your Future*

Micah 2:11 "These people want the kind of prophet who goes around full of lies and deceit and says, 'I prophesy that wine and liquor will flow for you.'"

Sorry, but this is just not the reality. Life is not going to be perfect for you; there is always a chance for disaster! No matter what you do or how you live, trials are always sure to come. That's life! Nobody is perfect; we all have sin, and we all need an adjustment every now and again. We all have our faith tested, but what a blessing to know the Lord will protect you, He will save you!

Micah 4:10 "You will have to go to Babylon, but there the Lord will save you from your enemies."

Ancient Babylon was located in modern day Iraq and was known to be a rebellious city which worshipped pagan gods, built the Tower of Babel, and was full of sexual immorality. The prophets mention Babylon as both a warning of punishment for Israel and an example of what displeases God. The New Testament portrays Babylon as a symbol of man's sinfulness and God's judgment. To say, "You will still have to go to Babylon," means there is a need for us "good people" to go through tough battles, this is a place displeasing to God, and it may not always be clear why we must go, but one thing is for sure, "there the Lord will save you from your enemies." So don't reject Him because you don't understand it, keep the Lord near, and He will save you from your enemies.

Life is never going to be all sunshine and rainbows; with the enemy being the prince of this world, and people having free will and choice to live against the Word of God and do evil unto others, there will always be hurt and pain of all kinds. You can surely bet you will continue to go through trials, but if you *live* in a place of righteousness with the Lord, He will be there by your side; He will bring you peace to get through it and He will save you from your enemies.

Acts 14:22 "[Paul and Barnabas] strengthened the believers and encouraged them to remain true to the faith. 'We must pass through many troubles to enter the Kingdom of God' they taught."

We must pass through *many* troubles! So be prepared! Build up your strength! Know the Word, know who you are, know the authority you carry and know that God is fighting with you and He is *for* you! Equip yourself with the armor of God! Strengthen your mind to not give up the faith when things get tough. And pray! Pray without ceasing! Pray even when things are looking up. Even if everything is perfect, pray!

How to Deal: *With Your Future*

Ephesians 6:10-20 "Finally, build up your strength in union with the Lord and by means of His mighty power. Put on all the armor that God gives you, so that you will be able to stand up against the devil's evil tricks. For we are not fighting against human beings but against the wicked spiritual forces in the Heavenly world, the rulers, authorities, and cosmic powers of this dark age. So put on God's armor now! Then when the evil day comes, you will be able to resist the enemy's attacks; and after fighting to the end, you will still hold your ground. So stand ready, with truth as a belt tight around your waist, with righteousness as your breastplate, and as your shoes the readiness to announce the Good News of peace. At all times carry faith as a shield; for with it you will be able to put out all the burning arrows shot by the Evil One. And accept salvation as a helmet, and the Word of God as the sword which the Spirit gives you. Do all this in prayer, asking for God's help. Pray on every occasion, as the Spirit leads. For this reason keep alert and never give up; pray always for all God's people. And pray also for me, that God will give me a message when I am ready to speak, so that I may speak boldly and make known the gospel's secret. For the sake of this gospel I am an ambassador, though now I am in prison. Pray that I may be bold in speaking about the gospel as I should."

You can never be too prepared. This joker is always looking for an open door to attack you. Don't let the attack discourage you, God can use it! That is why prayer is a lifestyle. When you don't know what to pray, pray in the Spirit; you never know what attacks may be lurking around the corner. Sin opens doors for the enemy to attack, keep those doors closed!

This is what I think people tend to get messed up, God does not provide instruction on how to live righteously just to make life hard to live and give us a standard on which to be judged and judge others, He provides instruction for our protection; don't murder, why? Not for a standard on which to shame and judge those who murder, but there are consequences, you go to prison, you deal with guilt and shame, someone else's family is torn apart, they want revenge, they come after you, and so on. Don't covet your neighbor's wife, why? Because she is already taken, and lust eventually turns into infatuation which turns into action and breaking up a marriage has its own repercussions, angry husband, devastated children, crimes of passion, etc. Don't have sex before marriage, why? Simple – soul ties. Say you have sex with Justin and you are absolutely sure he will be your husband, you have even talked about it with him and he's all in so it's as good as done, right? Wrong. Now you begin to realize Justin is a psychopath and you surely can't spend a life with a psychopath, or Justin discovers something he doesn't like much about you or worse, he finds someone else he likes more and leaves you. What now? You try to move on, you find a nice guy that you can start a family with but, you have this deep connection with Justin, he's always there in the back of your mind. Sure, Tom is great, he loves you, he's a great dad, he's always there for you, but Justin…

So again, these laws or instructions are not to hurt you, they are only for your benefit. Resist sin, not to prove you are righteous, not to judge others for not doing as well as you, but for you. Stand firm in the faith!

1 Peter 5:8-9 "Be alert, be on watch! Your enemy, the devil, roams around like a roaring lion, looking for someone to devour. Be firm in your faith and resist him, because you know that other believers in all the world are going through the same kind of sufferings."

Things might look good now but remain alert. You may think with your "luck", its only a matter of time before you lose it all again. You may look around and it may seem like everyone else has their life together and everything is always perfect for everyone else and you're the only one who ever struggles, but we all suffer.

Matthew 10:16-20 "I am sending you out just like sheep to a pack of wolves. You must be as cautious as snakes and as gentle as doves. Watch out, for there will be those who will arrest you and take you to court, and they will whip you in the synagogues. For My sake you will be brought to trial before rulers and kings, to tell the Good News to them and to the Gentiles. When they bring you to trial, do not worry about

Prepare for Disaster

what you are going to say or how you will say it; when the time comes, you will be given what you will say. For the words you will speak will not be yours; they will come from the Spirit of your Father speaking through you."

The spirit speaks, through us, things we can never know; not only in prayer, but when we rely on Him to speak through us in the midst of trials. The Holy Spirit is wisdom, so praying in the Spirit is the best defense we have to prepare to defend us from the unknown attacks. This is why we need to pray without ceasing, as the Bible says. If we pray only when we see the adversity, then we're already in it; but if we pray in the Spirit continually, He can help us to avoid the unnecessary pains of life, while giving us the strength to make it through the inevitable.

Luke 21:36 "Be on watch and pray always that you will have the strength to go safely through all those things that will happen and to stand before the Son of Man."

Pray now for strength for the future. Just because everything looks good now, scripture says those things *will* happen; start pray-paring now! God has already equipped you with all you need to defeat the enemy. You have your armor; you just need to use it. Don't fear your enemies, but pray, because it is never us who defeats him anyway, God does.

How to Deal: *With Your Future*

Philippians 1:28-29 "Don't be afraid of your enemies; always be courageous, and this will prove to them that they will lose and that you will win, because it is God who gives you the victory."

For non-Christians, it is often the trouble and struggle that brings them to God, so why as seasoned Christians, does the struggle make us want to turn away and lose our faith in God? We already know He is the only one who can save us, so why do we blame Him and turn away as if He doesn't have another plan in play? Just because we have this relationship with God doesn't excuse us from disaster; it only means that He will be with us through it and bring us victory in the end.

John 16:31-33 "Jesus answered them, 'Do ye now believe? Behold, the hour cometh, yea, is now come, that ye shall be scattered, every man to his own, and shall leave me alone: and yet I am not alone, because the Father is with me. These things I have spoken unto you, that in me ye might have peace. In the world ye shall have tribulation: but be of good cheer; I have overcome the world.'" -KJV

Chapter 12

Praise God with Thanksgiving

Psalm 34:1-22 "I will praise the Lord at all times. I will constantly speak His praises. I will boast only in the Lord; let all who are helpless take heart. Come, let us tell of the Lord's greatness; let us exalt His Name together. I prayed to the Lord, and He answered me. He freed me from all my fears. Those who look to Him for help will be radiant with joy; no shadow of shame will darken their faces. In my desperation I prayed, and the Lord listened; He saved me from all my troubles. For the angel of the Lord is a guard; he surrounds and defends all who fear Him. Taste and see that the Lord is good Oh, the joys of those who take refuge in Him! Fear the Lord, you His godly people, for those who fear Him will have all they need. Even strong young lions sometimes go hungry, but those who trust in the Lord will lack no good thing. Come, my children, and listen to me, and I will teach you to fear the Lord. Does anyone want to live a life that is long and prosperous? Then keep your tongue from speaking evil and your lips from telling lies! Turn away from evil and do good. Search for peace, and work to maintain it. The eyes of the Lord watch over those who do right; His ears are open to their cries for help. But the Lord turns His face against those who do evil; He will erase their memory from the earth. The Lord hears His people when they call to Him for help. He rescues them from all their troubles. The Lord is close to the brokenhearted; He rescues those whose spirits are crushed. The righteous person faces many troubles, but the Lord comes to the rescue each time. For the Lord protects the bones of the righteous; not one of them is broken! Calamity will surely destroy the wicked, and those who hate the righteous will be punished. But the Lord will redeem those who serve Him. No one who takes refuge in Him will be condemned. Zechariah 10:11 "When they pass through their sea of trouble, I, the Lord, will strike the waves, and the depths of the Nile will go dry. — I will make My people strong; they will worship and obey Me.' The Lord has spoken."

Praise God! This is what it was all for! He has known from the beginning that you were going to pass through the trouble, because He's the one who clears the path for you! His intention is that *when* you come out, you will be stronger for it and you will know *His* strength, ability, love, and power, and you will worship and obey Him. He works *all* things together *for our good.* I have heard people cringe at the idea of "worship and obey" when it comes to God, perhaps it is because they've never truly acknowledged the great things He has done and still does for us daily or perhaps it's because they cannot physically see Him that causes some disconnect.

I think about it like this, for many people, there's an artist they like who writes songs that reach a special place for them which gets them through tough times, Beyonce, Taylor Swift, Harry Styles, etc. They in turn idolize this artist and worship them, they follow them on all social media accounts, they have their pictures on their wall or their wallpaper on their phone, they spend their money on tickets to see them perform and hear the same songs they've heard a hundred million times. They scream, they cry, they faint at the sight of them, they would lay down their lives and do absolutely anything in the world for them. Why? Why them and not God? He has done infinitely more for you than write a couple catchy lyrics that resonate with you. He literally gave you life, literally laid down His own, and literally knows you and loves you. Look for Him, He's always there. It is okay to worship and obey Him, He deserves it all.

It can be easy to obey God when you've never been through really tough times. It can be tough to obey God when you've gone through tough times alone, without Him. It's one thing to obey God when you've never truly seen what

He can do – when you've only heard testimony from others; but when you have your own first-hand experience of what God has done in *your* life, there's nothing else like it! You'll know Him on a whole other level. You will know to run to Him and turn your face to Him in times of trouble; it will be nothing to worship Him freely.

The troubles will pass, and God will deliver us from this season; we will come out stronger and victorious. Though it may feel like you are in a sea of trouble, surrounded on all sides with no land in sight, God will perform miracles on your behalf; He will strike the waves and at a moment's notice you will find yourself on dry land. He will get you through your season of trouble in an instant, and all He expects in return is your worship and obedience! That's it!

Ephesians 5:20 "In the name of our Lord Jesus Christ, always give thanks for everything to God the Father."

I know I never could have made it through what I made it through and how I made it through it without God. He brought me every single victory, so I give Him thanks for *everything*. All through this journey, He has brought me from darkness to light. Every step of the way He has done things for me that I could have never made happen for myself. I've done nothing to deserve any of it!

Colossians 1:12 "And with joy give thanks to the Father, who has made you fit to have your share of what God has reserved for His people in the Kingdom of light."

The thing that we must remember is that as good as we may try to be, we all have a sinful nature. None of us are worthy of God's goodness in any measure; but it is Him who makes us fit to share what God has reserved for us in *His* goodness and mercy. There is nothing we could ever do to qualify outside of Him. That is why we honor Him and give *Him* all the praise.

Isaiah 25:1-5 "Lord, you are my God; I will honor you and praise Your name. You have done amazing things; You have faithfully carried out the plans You made long ago. You have turned cities into ruins and destroyed their fortifications. The palaces which our enemies built are gone forever. The people of powerful nations will praise You; You will be feared in the cities of cruel nations. The poor and the helpless have fled to You and have been safe in times of trouble. You give them shelter from storms and shade from the burning heat. Cruel enemies attack like a winter storm, like drought in a dry land. But You, Lord, have silenced our enemies; You silence the shouts of cruel people, as a cloud cools a hot day."

Consider all He has done each and every day; everything He has kept you from and keeps from you! Consider His goodness and glory. Consider His protection when you had no idea that you needed protection at all! Give thankfulness for the negative moments of your past that in His infinite ability, He removed or plucked away the shame as if it never existed. To God be the glory!

Psalm 119:164 "Seven times each day I thank you for your righteous judgments."

Now I will admit, I'm not always quite as creative when thinking of God's goodness as Isaiah 25:1-5; sometimes I have a hard time being thankful *once* a day, let alone *seven!* But after all I've been through on this journey, I have learned one thing, my faith in God gives me a peace I can always be thankful for and rejoice over.

Proverbs 3:23-26 "You can go safely on your way and never even stumble. You will not be afraid when you go to bed, and you will sleep soundly through the night. You will not have to worry about sudden disasters, such as come on the wicked like a storm. The Lord will keep you safe. He will not let you fall into a trap."

Praise God with Thanksgiving

The storms will come, but even then, I can have peace knowing that just as He's done before, He will keep me safe every time! Whether I am in need or have more than enough, I can call on the Holy Spirit for guidance and He will get me through. God is so good! In the storms, just as the Bible states, He has given me the perfect peace, the peace that surpasses all understanding. And moreover, God wants to cover *you* with that peace in your own storms of life! Hallelujah!

Philippians 4:11-13 "And I am not saying this because I feel neglected, for I have learned to be satisfied with what I have. I know what it is to be in need and what it is to have more than enough. I have learned this secret, so that anywhere, at any time, I am content, whether I am full or hungry, whether I have too much or too little. I have the strength to face all conditions by the power that Christ gives me."

Have you learned this secret? To be content and trust in God no matter what the situation looks like? Our trials teach us to be stronger in our faith. Apostle Paul wrote the Book of Philippians, addressing the Church of Philippi, while in *prison*. Paul was encouraging the church from a place of imprisonment to work out their differences and have faith and to believe in Jesus Christ. Paul is expressing to be content at all times, concerning your walk in Christ.

How to Deal: *With Your Future*

Colossians 2:6-7 "Since you have accepted Christ Jesus as Lord, live in union with Him. Keep your roots deep in Him, build your lives on Him, and become stronger in your faith, as you were taught. And be filled with thanksgiving."

Many times, it seems like a daunting task to live in union with Christ. Surely, building your life on faith is no easy feat, especially when we tend to seek to know every detail about every step of everything and have control of our future and destiny. But what if we've got it all backwards? Building your life on faith, walking with Him, and being a thankful child of God pleases Him and He rewards those who please Him. Focus everyday in union with God, providing thanksgiving and praise, and your relationship will grow deeper in Him and He will reward you for it.

Ecclesiastes 2:26 "God gives wisdom, knowledge, and happiness to those who please Him, but He makes sinners work, earning and saving, so that what they get can be given to those who please Him."

So, you mean to tell me that all I have to do is relax and trust in Him and He will provide without me having to work, earn and save as the sinners do? *That's* the kind of promises God has for me if I just chill and trust Him for everything? Yes! Yield to all the ways and wisdom of God, you don't have to toil in the earth for things He wants to freely provide for you! Praise Him for it! But don't just praise Him when you've received something, praise Him because of who He is not simply because of what He gives. As much as we have sinned, He still gave His Son for us. He is our defender, protector, redeemer...Praise Him! He has redeemed us from the Law of Moses given to us for the sins of Adam. That, alone, is enough!

Romans 5:18 "So then, as the one sin condemned all people, in the same way the one righteous act sets all people free and gives them life."

If He never did anything else for us in this lifetime, Jesus gave His life for us so that we as sinners could receive salvation, grace, and freedom from the Law of Moses. As good as people have been or could ever be to you, how many would give up their life for a sinner? Especially now in this "cancel culture," you see a sinner these days, or simply a good person who makes a simple mistake and we're quick to call for the end of their entire being! But as quickly as we judge, Jesus is just as quick to love and forgive them and He still gave His life even for that one sinner.

Romans 5:7-8 "It is a difficult thing for someone to die for a righteous person. It may even be that someone might dare to die for a good person. But God has shown us how much He loves us — it was while we were still sinners that Christ died for us!"

Think about the lowest, dirtiest, death row deserving inmate who is one hundred percent guilty of committing absolutely unspeakable acts. We say, death! But Jesus says, life! Even until their last breath, He desires their salvation. Even if they were the only sinner in existence, Jesus died for him to have life! He laid down His life so that we might be in union with Him, He alone makes us worthy to receive every spiritual blessing in Heaven.

Ephesians 1:3 "Let us give thanks to the God and Father of our Lord Jesus Christ! For in our union with Christ He has blessed us by giving us every spiritual blessing in the Heavenly world."

It doesn't say "because of how good we are, He has blessed us…" It's not because of *us,* it's not because of what we do. It is because of *Him* that He *has blessed* us by giving us every spiritual blessing in the Heavenly world. He has already blessed us; He has already given! We just have to know it and receive it! He *wants* us to be blessed! He *wants* us to rule with Him in Heaven!

Ephesians 2:6 "In our union with Christ Jesus He raised us up with Him to rule with Him in the Heavenly world."

Praise God with Thanksgiving

In the earth God makes us the head and not the tail, as He designed us to reign and rule with Him in dominion, authority, and power which he has bequeath to us! When we really begin to understand this, we can get to the point of appreciating even our suffering. That is the point of real spiritual maturity.

Colossians 1:24 "And now I am happy about my sufferings for you, for by means of my physical sufferings I am helping to complete what still remains of Christ's sufferings on behalf of His body, the church."

When you truly trust God, you can be thankful for the process even through suffering. The awareness of personal suffering and being content and thankful in the process is a challenge for us all in the flesh, however when we consider the atoning ransom price He paid for us, our suffering with Him is all worth it! He's got a plan for it.

Matthew 5:3-10 "Blessed are the poor in spirit, for theirs is the Kingdom of Heaven. Blessed are those who mourn, for they will be comforted. Blessed are the meek, for they will inherit the earth. Blessed are those who hunger and thirst for righteousness, for they will be filled. Blessed are the merciful, for they will be shown mercy. Blessed are the pure in heart, for they will see God. Blessed are the peacemakers, for they will be called children of God. Blessed are those who are persecuted, for theirs is the Kingdom of Heaven."

This scripture is titled *True Happiness* in which case it would appear, we've got it entirely backwards. The "poor in spirit" and the "persecuted" are blessed because God blesses the marginalized and rights the wrongs done here on earth, "blessed are the meek" because as we know God blessed the humble and they inherit the earth, and He resists the proud. But the most interesting to me, is "blessed are those who mourn, for they will be comforted" to me, the blessing is that, even when we mourn, God's comfort in mourning is far greater than simply walking in a state of ease.

It's hard to explain if you've never experienced it but, it's like the difference between taking a bath after laying around all day and taking a bath after a rough day at work. Does that make sense? A relaxing bath feels so much better after you've put your body through the wringer at work all day. A relaxing bath after a relaxing day is just, meh. It's alright. So, it's not that we *seek* the mourning, but we can have confidence through it, that He still has a plan, His comfort is there, it is good, there is nothing like it! God comforts us and shares His glory with us through Christ.

Colossians 1:27 "God's plan is to make known His secret to His people, this rich and glorious secret which He has for all peoples. And

Praise God with Thanksgiving

the secret is that Christ is in you, which means that you will share in the glory of God."

If you consider the glory of God, which is so great that man cannot even look upon His face, people would quit selling their souls to the devil for fame and start seeking this glory that is freely available to us who believe in Him, which is far greater! The enemy will sell you out in a second, but the Lord will never leave you nor forsake you. His desire for you is always good and for your good.

Isaiah 41:17-20 "When My people in their need look for water, when their throats are dry with thirst, then I, the Lord, will answer their prayer; I, the God of Israel, will never abandon them. I will make rivers flow among barren hills and springs of water run in the valleys. I will turn the desert into pools of water and the dry land into flowing springs. I will make cedars grow in the desert, and acacias and myrtles and olive trees. Forests will grow in barren land, forests of pine and juniper and cypress. People will see this and know that I, the Lord, have done it. They will come to understand that Israel's holy God has made it happen."

God wants to bless you, but He wants the glory! He wants to prosper you in all ways, but He wants the glory. If you turn to Him in need of a drink, He will give you that and much more! He will take your need and turn it into abundance. He will take your little and make it more than enough. Give Him glory!!

Matthew 14:19-21 "[Jesus] took the five loaves and the two fish, looked up to Heaven, and gave thanks to God. He broke the loaves and gave them to the disciples, and the disciples gave them to the people. Everyone ate and had enough. Then the disciples took up twelve baskets full of what was left over. The number of men who ate was about five thousand, not counting the women and children."

When Jesus performed this miracle of multiplication, He didn't take what He had and ration it out sparingly – first come first served; He didn't pray for more, He didn't even ask God to multiply it. He simply gave thanks to God for the little He had, and God did the rest. This is what happens when you give thanks to God. He knows what we need, and He desires to give it to us, we simply need to do our part and be thankful.

John 17:1 "After Jesus finished saying this, He looked up to Heaven and said, 'Father, the hour has come, give glory to Your Son, so that the Son may give glory to You.'"

Here Jesus was asking God to "glorify Him" by sending Him to death on the cross, so that His mission on earth would be made known or glorified. He *asked* for the cross, the complete suffering and utter humiliation, for the purpose of bringing glory to the Father. That is the purpose Jesus was sent to the earth to fulfill, that is the purpose we all carry. We may not ask for our suffering, but it's coming is inevitable, and we *can* have the right perspective of it and bring God glory in it.

"Glorify" was one of John's favorite expressions concerning what would happen to Jesus as a result of His crucifixion and resurrection. In His deepest suffering, Jesus was brought into His glory with the Father in a new way, as the crucified and risen Lord, Jesus Christ. Jesus knew this glory belonged to Him, it was His promise, so He called out to the Father asking for what was already His. It's that simple.

People often make God far more complicated than He is, when in reality it all boils down to one thing, love God and each other. In doing those things, you *have* fulfilled the whole Law. The Pharisees will try and try to convince you there's more to it, but when you love God, you give thanks for what He's done, you trust Him, you keep His Word. When you love others, you don't murder them, you don't steal from them, you don't covet their spouse, etc.

How to Deal: *With Your Future*

Matthew 5:20 "I tell you, then, that you will be able to enter the Kingdom of Heaven only if you are more faithful than the teachers of the Law and the Pharisees in doing what God requires."

The Pharisees did not play around when it came to obeying the Law, unfortunately their efforts were misguided. God wants us to be even more diligent than they were, but in doing as *He* requires. He sent us Jesus so that things would be *different*. Be diligent in gratitude, in love and in relationship with Him.

He doesn't ask for much, truly He doesn't. Sometimes it even seems meaningless because it is so simple; but it means absolutely everything to Him. It is not as difficult as people have made it seem in the past, and that is why I believe people are so confused about God and what it takes to be "right" with Him. That is why it is so important to be your own advocate; know the Word for yourself, don't depend on traditions handed down, be more faithful than teachers of the Law and Pharisees. You don't need a theology degree or a lifetime of church experience to know the truth of the Lord.

Matthew 11:25-26 "Jesus said, 'Father, Lord of Heaven and earth! I thank You because You have shown to the unlearned what You have hidden from the wise and learned. Yes, Father, this was how You were pleased to have it happen."

God is funny that way. He will reveal more to a new believer than someone who has spent their entire life in the church. Why? Often times people who grew up in the church are so convinced of what they have been taught that they will argue even against the Word of God itself. The truth is, God will reveal what He wants to reveal to those He wants to reveal it to. You may feel inferior to those more experienced, but you can always confirm it with the scriptures; have confidence, He is no respecter of persons. God is seeking someone who will listen, not simply read what was written. A relationship with the Father will reveal far more than a Bible study. Knowing the Word of God is great, it is important, but it is nothing without relationship.

Matthew 12:5-7 "Or have you not read in the Law of Moses that every Sabbath the priests in the Temple actually break the Sabbath law, yet they are not guilty? I tell you that there is something here greater than the Temple. The scripture says, 'It is kindness that I want, not animal sacrifices.'"

Some people use the scriptures to be mean and condemn others. That was never God's intention. What God wants and what He sent His Son here for, is love and kindness; that is the new Law that Jesus came to bring us, and we still can't seem to get it right.

Romans 12:10 "Love one another warmly as Christians, and be eager to show respect for one another."

There is a way to speak to one another respectfully as Christians. Our theology may not line up, but there is only one source of truth, and that is the Word of God, and if we can agree on that and meet on love then we can respectfully get along.

Matthew 15:2-3 & 8-9 "'Why is it that Your disciples disobey the teaching handed down by our ancestors? They don't wash their hands in the proper way before they eat!' Jesus answered, 'And why do you disobey God's command and follow your own teaching?' — 'These people,' says God, 'honor Me with their words, but their heart is really far away from Me. It is no use for them to worship Me, because they teach human rules as though they were My laws!'"

God's Word is what matters, not what you have been taught. Anything outside of kindness and love is outside of God. At this point He really couldn't care less about the rituals and sacrifices, He doesn't *want* you following the teachings of your ancestors, He wants your simple obedience to the one Law of Love and keeping your heart close to Him.

Praise God with Thanksgiving

Romans 1:25 "They exchanged the truth about God for a lie, and worshipped and served created things rather than the Creator-who is forever praised. Amen."

Don't exchange the truth of God's Word for anything *anyone* says. Don't worship and serve the traditions of man. Study the teachings left by those who walked with Jesus, who have the wisdom. You will be glad if you can remember them so you cannot be swayed.

Proverbs 22:17 "listen, and I will teach you what the wise have said. Study their teachings, and you will be glad if you remember them and can quote them."

My desire with this book was always to reach the unbeliever, as I once was. The church is already being preached to, and I don't desire to add my two cents. But the experiences the Lord has given me, tough as they were, I believe they have the power and purpose to speak into the lives of people like me, and that is all I can hope to come of this.

Romans 15:20 "My ambition has always been to proclaim the Good News in places where Christ has not been heard of, so as not to build on a foundation laid by someone else."

How to Deal: *With Your Future*

As I have stated in the beginning, I am nobody, I have no spiritual training or designation, I didn't grow up in the church, but I have something I think many people are lacking in the church today, and that is a relationship with the Lord which allows me to love others and be kind. I pray that the revelation of this truth will fix hurts caused in others the way it was in me, and I pray that we can all choose love above anything else.

1 Peter 1:22 "Now that by your obedience to the truth you have purified yourselves and have come to have a sincere love for other believers, love one another earnestly with all your heart."

To have the love of God doesn't mean to love the lovable, but to love everyone, even when it's hard. I have been falsely accused, betrayed, backstabbed, and torn apart by people I loved and brought into my life and circle, and I chose to love them through it. It was not easy, it never is, but it is what God requires, and He will get us through it.

1 Thessalonians 5:14-19 "We urge you, our friends, to warn the idle, encourage the timid, help the weak, be patient with everyone. See that no one pays back wrong for wrong, but at all times make it your aim to do good to one another and to all people. Be joyful always, pray at all times,

Praise God with Thanksgiving

be thankful in all circumstances. This is what God wants from you in your life in union with Christ Jesus."

Whatever you give to Him, He will work it out for you far better than you ever could. People will continue to betray us, no matter how good we treat them, it's in their nature. So, remember this one thing - praise God. Give it to Him and shout for joy and rejoice! Because God has it all in His hands.

Zephaniah 3:14-17 "Sing and shout for joy, - rejoice with all your heart, - the Lord has stopped your punishment; He has removed all your enemies. The Lord, the King of Israel, is with you; there is no reason now to be afraid. – The Lord your God is with you; His power gives you victory. The Lord will take delight in you, and in His love He will give you new life."
Proverbs 30:5 "God keeps every promise He makes. He is like a shield for all who seek His protection."

As I sit writing the final words of this book from my balcony overlooking the beauty of the ocean, God's creation, I can't help but look back, so glad I never gave up, so glad I kept the faith, so glad I trusted in Him. His promises were true, He kept His word! If I had given up, I would have never known. I'm so glad I made it.

"I give thanks to Christ Jesus our Lord, who has given me strength for my work. I thank Him for considering me worthy and appointing me to serve Him, even though in the past I spoke evil of Him and persecuted and insulted Him. But God was merciful to me because I did not yet have faith and so did not know what I was doing."
                                                                    -1 Timothy 1:12-13

Praise God with Thanksgiving

Micah 7:8 "We have fallen, but we will rise again. We are in darkness now, but the Lord will give us Light."

How to Deal: *With Your Future*

Made in the USA
Columbia, SC
12 March 2023

13581195R00193